Daddy's Girl

DEBORAH WATLING

Daddy's Girl

THE AUTOBIOGRAPHY

Written with Paul W.T. Ballard

fantom
publishing

First published in 2010 by Fantom Films
fantomfilms.co.uk

A catalogue record for this book is available from the British Library.

Hardback Edition ISBN: 978-1-906263-40-9
Standard Paperback Edition ISBN: 978-1-906263-41-6

Typeset by Phil Reynolds Media Services, Leamington Spa
Printed by MPG Biddles Limited, King's Lynn

Front cover image © Bill Zygmant/Rex Features
Back cover image © Paul W.T. Ballard and Dexter O'Neill

Photographs appear on plates between pages 74 and 75 and
between pages 138 and 139. All photographs not specifically credited
are from the author's personal collection.

Contents

Foreword

It really is hard to believe that it is well over forty years since I first met Victoria Waterfield, better known to you and me as Deborah Watling; but even better known to me, with great affection, if she will forgive me, as Debbie. It was 1967, and I had been invited to hang around the *Doctor Who* rehearsal rooms in London, and the usual recording at Lime Grove on Saturday evenings. *The Evil of the Daleks* was, of course, Debbie's baptism into the family of the Doctor, even though that family was quite young in those early years of the show.

Forgive me if I spend a few moments of your time looking back at that young gal, with the most beautiful large blue eyes; a gal who has enchanted television viewers and stage audiences for a very long time. Of course we think of her here as such a part of a long-running television science fiction series; but in fact Debbie's career spans so many plays, films, and television roles that it is hard to pick and choose those I like best. But coming from such a distinguished and lovable family as the Watlings, it is no wonder that over the years so much talent has oozed from this hard-working actress. I remember her dad, Jack Watling, telling me once that he had no idea where

1

his daughters and son got their talent from. "The only thing I can think is that, unlike a lot of actors these days, they do their homework!"

Debbie has always done her homework, that's for sure. A few years back, I remember going to see her in a pantomime at the Cambridge Arts Theatre – *Dick Whittington*, in which she played a character called Fairy Bowbells. What about that for a name! Well, she carried it off with wonderful comic composure, despite the constant teasing from leading artist, Barry Cryer. The thing about successful comedy is that you play it for real, and Debbie always knew how to do that. And her timing is impeccable. I particularly remember several moments in a film in which she starred opposite Cliff Richard, called *Take Me High*. It was a domestic scene in which the two of them were cooking hamburgers in the kitchen and singing one of Cliff's songs as a duet. But what was so fascinating was not only my surprise to discover that Debbie had such a good singing voice, but that she handled her co-star with such confidence. And boy, was that final kiss sexy! If only Victoria Waterfield had seen *that*!

Of course, Debbie has had to tolerate quite a lot of teasing over her rather long career. I don't think I need elaborate on the practical jokes played on her by her two *Who* companions, Patrick Troughton and Frazer Hines; they are by now legend. But I myself haven't been all that kind to her. There was an occasion once at a *Who* convention in Southampton when she, Jack Watling and myself were on stage, when Debbie was asked by someone in the audience if she had any good ideas for a *Who* story. She replied that "as a matter of fact I have." However, as she launched into the most complicated plot for a new *Who* story, Jack and I, sitting just behind her on stage, immediately closed our eyes and pretended to fall asleep, amidst loud, deafening snores. We paid the price for *that* particular tease, I can tell you! But as always, Debbie took it all in her stride, and enjoyed the fun alongside everyone else.

What really gives me a warm glow is to know that Debbie has had a loving life, both with her husband and her family. Every time I see her at a convention or on stage, I've often wondered why she is so endearing to her audiences. Is it because of that diminutive frame, or those appealing blue eyes, or the voice that can sound just as sexy as it can loudly yell when it is trying to kill off the seaweed creatures in *Fury from the Deep*? But in the end I've come to the decision that it is because Debbie is such a consummate artiste: someone who knows how to move and speak like the character she is portraying.

Of course I'm very proud to know Debbie as a personal friend. Although we only ever seem to meet at conventions, when we do eventually get a few quiet moments together it's as though the years have rolled back and we can talk the same language about all the things and people we like and don't like, both professionally and in our personal lives. On these rare occasions, it's always great to be with her.

I suppose my most abiding memory of Debbie is her farewell to the Doctor and Jamie in the final episode of my own *Fury from the Deep* for *Doctor Who*. She had so much lying ahead of her, so much to do to follow in the proud tradition of her family, so many boards to tread, so many camera lenses in which to be focused, so many writers' scripts to learn. And d'you know what? I think she's memorised her lines pretty well over the years, don't you? How many giggles we'll never know, how many "fluffs" we'll never know. But what we *do* know is that, over the years, she has done her homework admirably, more than her dad or anyone else would have dared hope. Maybe that's why we all love and admire "Daddy's Girl" so much.

Victor Pemberton
March 2010

Prologue

There are some things in life which remain completely the same, no matter how the years go by. Not so long ago I was approached by BBC Radio 4 to go back to Snowdonia to record a documentary on the locations used for the *Doctor Who* story *The Abominable Snowmen*. Forty years had passed since the cameras had stopped rolling, and we'd all trundled into the old rattling coaches to head back to London. Tired, full of excitement, but still bursting with energy.

I don't quite know what I was expecting to find when I went back. In so many ways I was an older, wiser woman than the sparky young girl I was when I'd last been there. But the surroundings were exactly as I remembered seeing them through my nineteen-year-old eyes. The cave where we'd uncovered the dreaded Yeti was obstinately perched halfway up the hill; and then there was the view down to the valley below… well it still took my breath away. From my vantage point I could actually see the storms sweeping across the vast sprawling skyline. Dramatic, angry, curling clouds tearing towards me, minutes before the actual rain began.

Memory Lane can be a strange and alluring place for one to go, but a painful one at times too. I smiled at the memories of larking around filming, being hugged by Yetis to keep warm, Pat and Frazer cracking jokes, working with Dad… My father had by this time passed away, and I sat there up on the hill with the rush of wind blowing through my hair, and the peace of a cool breeze on my face, and remembered him. As I often do.

The storm passed overhead, and in the valley below the sunshine began to break through the darkened clouds.

Chapter One

"**D**aughter of Jack…" has been used so often in the press whenever I am discussed. And I don't mind one bit because my father was a great star of stage and screen. During his career he made more than fifty movies, including timeless war classics such as *We Dive at Dawn*, *The Way Ahead*, *Sink the Bismarck*… the list is endless. But he didn't actually envisage becoming an actor. These days nearly everyone wants to be famous for something, but Dad was born in Walthamstow and raised in Chingford, and only developed theatrical aspirations after a trip to Stratford to see a Shakespeare production. He'd previously seen Laurence Olivier play Hamlet at London's Old Vic and been more impressed by the buskers outside, but now suddenly felt a calling to the acting world.

He flunked secretarial college and trained at the prestigious Italia Conti School of Acting, making his West End debut in *Once A Crook* in 1939. He actually told a white lie to Equity to gain membership: adding to his age so he could get on with his career! His breakthrough role came with a part in the Terence Rattigan play *Flare Path*, a play I myself appeared in many years later. With the country at war, Father wanted to do his bit and enrolled in the RAF, training as a navigator. Although he trained successfully, he was let down by his eyesight, and couldn't take up the position. In the end he was posted to the film unit with Richard Attenborough, making films to help morale during the conflict.

My mother, Patricia Hicks, was a film actress with experience of the stage both on Broadway and in the West End. She was married before the war, but sadly her husband was killed in an accident, leaving her widowed with a daughter, Dilys. Dilys is in fact my stepsister, as Daddy adopted her, but I have never thought of her as a stepsister at all; she's my big sister. It wasn't long after the war that Mother and Father met each other, as they were both acting in different plays in London at the time.

It was George Cole who spotted her first, rather excitedly saying to Father:

"You've got to come and see this bit of crumpet in the Park!"

Mother was playing Hermia in an open-air production of *A Midsummer Night's Dream* at Regent's Park, whilst Daddy was in *The Winslow Boy* at the Lyric Theatre. He was the debonair young matinée idol, and set about wooing her immediately. He succeded, despite the attempts of one unscrupulous friend who told Mummy not to bother with him because he was gay! Father happily disproved this when he gave her a lift home one evening, staged a breakdown in Epping Forest and pounced.

Family legend goes that I was conceived in the number two dressing room: proof, if any were needed, that my origins are firmly theatrical. I was already on my way when Mummy and Daddy got married in summer 1947, which meant that they actually had to tell people that I was premature when I made my debut in January the following year. Such was the stigma attached to sex before marriage, they even had to pretend to their families. I was born in Queen Charlotte's Hospital in London, which was a very grand place; everybody wanted to have their baby there in those days. Mother found it somewhat grim, however, and said that the nurses there were so strict and forboding that she didn't want to speak to them, and I just sort of popped out whilst they weren't around.

Father always maintained that Mother was better at acting than he was, and joked at how he thought that, once he'd married her, he'd be able to retire and live off her roles. Mummy shattered this illusion early on by confidently stating, "Here's my daughter, here's my mum, we're all moving and I'm going to quit the business." She didn't straight away, but did not long before I was born. She was appearing on Broadway in *Arsenic and Old Lace*, and started to get pernicious sickness. She couldn't even hold down water, and the stage started to spin around her. As a seasoned professional she made it through the run, but decided enough was enough when she got home and that was going to be it for her.

We asked her many times over the years to have another go, but Mother always refused, until a few years back when we were down for the summer at Frinton. We rented a cottage just outside town called Fourways and she agreed to do a part in the weekly rep. Everything had been going well during rehearsals in the week, but come the opening night she did a runner. The car had been parked on the drive one moment, and the next it was gone, with her in it.

"Daddy, she's gone; what are we going to do?" we asked.

"Don't worry, darlings," smiled Dad. "There's no petrol in the car. She'll be back."

She did come back and performed, but hated every minute of it. It took another fifteen years to persuade her back, once again at Frinton Summer Theatre. We all nervously turned up on the first night to support her through it. Giles, my brother, was also in the cast, but not playing a relation, which made it all the more surprising when halfway through the play she stood up, looked directly at him and announced:

"Come on son, we're going."

"I'm not your son in this one!" he whispered.

The crowd laughed appreciatively. I don't know how she made it through the week, but she did, and was terrible to live with because she was constantly on edge. That was the last time she performed. Never again.

~

We lived in Epping at Kendall Avenue in a house called The Oaks. There was Nanny and Granddad (my mother's parents), Father, Mother, myself and Dilys. We had various lodgers too who would come and stop for a while to supplement the income and help pay the mortgage. Father was always travelling back and forth into London to play in the West End, and Mother would often accompany him, so Nanny took charge of a great deal of day-to-day things and bringing up us children. Nanny was a great organiser. She was also always there for us. Not that Mummy and Daddy weren't; Father's career was thriving and Mother was usually on hand to offer support whilst he was away on tour or filming, so Nanny was a very solid constant in my life.

Nanny was a wonderfully quirky character. The girls at school used to love coming to tea because they liked Mum's salad with vinaigrette dressing, and so we had somebody round nearly every day. One day Nanny exclaimed:

"Why don't you go to your own houses, why do you come here? Why don't you take Debs round to your homes? We don't want you round here any more."

"How dare you say that to my friends!" I stormed.

"They're costing us a fortune," she fumed. "Why do you come here?"

"We like the house and we like being here… and we do like you."

"Oh all right," she said, melting instantly.

On another occasion Father was appearing in the West End and he decided to take the family and the cast of the show to the Savoy Grill for dinner after opening night to celebrate. Nan always wore her hat, everywhere, and she also loved wearing her big fur coat. The Savoy was, as it is still, a very pricey place to dine.

"Look at the price of this Jack," she exclaimed. "It's daylight robbery!"

Nan organised the waiters as if she was the manager; clicking her fingers and having them run around back and forth. They had brilliant service, and an excellent meal, but Nanny still wasn't impressed. She kept saying how expensive it all was and how they couldn't possibly justify the price. They finished the meal and were walking down the street when Father noticed Nanny was looking a bit plumper than she had done earlier.

"What's wrong with your coat?" he asked.

Nanny proudly peeled back the flaps of her coat to unveil a shining silver canteen of cutlery she'd pilfered from the Savoy. Mummy and Daddy where aghast.

"You haven't just stolen that?" said Mother, horrified.

"The prices they charge, they should expect it," Nanny replied, unabashed.

Nanny was the queen of amdram in Epping, but could be rather embarrassing in how she pushed you forward sometimes. She belonged to a Women's Institute and every year they would have an evening where you took your grandchild along; they would perform a song or recite a poem, the ladies would clap and coo, and it would all be very nice and everyone would be very proud. One year Nanny took me along to this event.

"Go on Debbie, go up and do a song for us," she said, ushering me onto the stage.

"Okay Nanny," I replied uncertainly.

I stood up on the stage and thought for a moment what I could sing. I wasn't very old, about five or so, and I suddenly remembered a song Dilys had taught me.

I looked out at the aged crowd with their big hats and blue rinses, then took a deep breath and launched into my little tune.

"Old Mrs Penny with a bamboo belly
And her tits tied up with string.
Sitting on the grass with her finger up her ass,
Singing God Save The Queen."

The jaws on the faces of the pensionable crowd dropped in horror and sheer disbelief. It wasn't my fault though! Dilys had taught it me, and I didn't realise it was rude!

Nanny took me abroad on holiday twice, which was a lovely treat: once when I was eight across the Bay of Biscay, via cargo ship, which was a cheaper way of doing it in those days. Then when I was sixteen she took me out to the Mediterranean to Greece, on a big liner, which was very grand, and I have lots of lovely photographs of the pair of us visiting the Acropolis. We dined every night on the ship, and I used to wear a very fetching backless dress, earning me the nicknames "Lolita" and "Jailbait" from the ship's crew!

My granddad always had one day a week in bed. He would sit there for the day with his pipe and not get up. Not for anything. One day when I was three, he came into the living room and looked at Mother.

"Right Pat," he declared. "I'm going to go to bed and I don't want to get up."

He went up the stairs, got into bed and just shut down. He had literally just given up, and within a week was dead. He had become tired of life, and didn't want to see even Nanny any more, just my mother. "Get my beauty," he would demand.

I always remember him smoking a pipe and pottering about in the garden. On one occasion he was cutting a holly bush, whilst smoking of course, and he actually set it on fire. He was a lovely gentle man, with a dry sense of humour, and he walked in through the back door puffing his pipe.

"Pat," he said, quite casually. "The holly bush is on fire."

"What!?" exclaimed Mother.

"The holly bush is on fire," he continued without an ounce of panic. "We'd better phone the fire brigade."

Dilys, ever the nutter, thought this was a brilliant opportunity for some fun. She's six years older than me, and was always up for some mischief. I can't have been any more than three years old; she bundled me into my pram and aimed me at the flaming holly bush. Mother caught sight of what was happening, let out a scream and saved me from my firey peril, much to Dilys's dismay.

I wasn't the sole target of my older sister's antics. She used to have a lovely boy who came round to play and have dinner. One day she took him into our garage and decided it would be fun to paint him from head to toe. With green emulsion paint. His mother was, as you can imagine, not best pleased. On another occasion she locked herself in the downstairs loo, and wouldn't come out.

"Come out at once, stop being silly," said Mother. "It's tea time soon, you can't stay in there forever."

Eventually she did, but it turned out she'd taken a carving knife from the kitchen and slashed the walls. Weird.

Despite such strangeness she always looked after me as a kid and was always on my side, protecting me. I have always had a mortal fear of dogs, ever since I was a child. Other people's dogs obviously, because I have had dogs of my own. Dilys decided she wanted to try and cure me of this phobia, and one day we were walking along Kendall Avenue when she spotted a man walking his Alsatian down the other side of the road.

"Awww," she cooed. "Let's go and pat the dog!"

Begrudgingly I let her drag me across the road.

"Isn't he lovely, come and stroke him."

"No, I don't want to," I replied rigidly.

"Look Debs, you've got to get over this dog thing," she said, organising me as ever.

She marched up to the pooch, rested her hand on his head, and it went for her, taking a chunk out of her leg. The screaming and the blood did little to cure my phobia, so I'm still terrified!

I used to hate going to school. I went to various different places, before I ended up at the convent school. Even then Dilys had to take me every day to make sure I went. I used to cling on screaming each morning, protesting that I wasn't going to go in. In retrospect I think she had to put up with a lot from me. Parkston was the name of the convent school, and the nuns there just left me alone. They assumed, given my family background, that there wasn't much point in trying to teach me anything because I was only going to become an actress at the end of it. Why would I need to know Boyle's Law or Pythagorus's Theorum? In some ways it was great.

"Excuse me sister," I would ask innocently, in the middle of a lesson. "Can I go out into the garden for a bit?"

"Of course you can Debbie!" they would smile.

It didn't teach me anything!

On the flipside, having the acting background meant that they were very keen on using me to enter singing competitions around the county. I was actually quite good, and used to come first or second, and the nuns were very proud. One song I recall singing when I was about eight was called Little Lucy Lavender.

"Little Lucy Lavender, aged just three,

Climbed up the apple tree…"

One of those very twee and very sweet little numbers, which I would perform cutely with all the actions. But the nuns loved it, and they loved me too. They were so excited when I won the part in *The Invisible Man* because they could see one of their girls on television. I got away with murder. Not that I was a badly behaved child: I was very good. Inwardly at any rate…

We had by this point moved away from Epping to Alderton Hall. There were many sad memories attached to our time at Epping, greatest of those being my little baby brother, Adam, who died there. I was three years old and Mummy took Adam out into the garden for his afternoon rest, to get some fresh air.

It had been snowing, and she left him outside under the eaves of the house. She popped back inside, and when she came out some snow had fallen from the roof above and smothered him. I was only three years old, but I can still vividly recall seeing my mother running past the kitchen window with Adam over her shoulder, his head lolling to one side. I was sat on the floor playing with my toys, and even at that age I knew he was dead.

Mother came crashing into the kitchen.

"Debbie, go to your room," she shouted.

I obeyed. I was always an obedient child.

Mother placed him down on the big farmhouse oak table that was in the centre of the kitchen, and tried with Nanny to revive him. But it was too late.

We were all distraught, but Mother especially as she blamed herself totally. She came to terms with it, but never got over it. There was no way she could have known what was going to happen; it was a tragic accident. Not that people in the town saw it that way. A small minority sent disgusting hate mail. Spiteful, nasty comments, which didn't help at all. Father was so concerned that he went to the doctor to see what he could do to assist, and the doctor said they should try for a new child straight away. Which they did, and nine months later along came Giles. They really wanted another boy, and God looked down and granted their wish.

From Epping we moved briefly to a small lodge in Buckhurst Hill, on one of the main roads. It was the lodge house to the main estate there, but was too cramped for the whole family to live in. Father wanted to buy a house in London, but couldn't find anything large enough. So for a while Mother, Father and Dilys went to stay in a property in London, whilst Nanny, myself and Giles went back to Epping to live with my best friend Cynthia Wooten. That meant that we were split up for a time, but used to visit London at weekend; me dragging a reluctant Giles along on the tube, then back off on the Sunday evening so we could be ready for school.

But it wasn't working, and Father soon realised that they would have to give up the house in London and look for something bigger outside. The London contingent came down to Epping for a change to stop with us one weekend, and Dilys, who was a mad keen horse girl, went out riding in the forest with Mother.

They were riding along quite happily, when all of a sudden there was a low hanging branch. Dilys ducked under it, but Mother didn't spot it and was whipped straight off her horse onto the ground below. She lay on the floor in agony, and it transpired later that she'd actually broken her collarbone.

"Don't worry Mummy, don't worry!" exclaimed Dilys. "I'll go and get some help!"

And off she shot into the undergrowth.

About twenty minutes later there was a rustling in the bushes, and out marched a passing troop of Boy Scouts with their leader. They were overjoyed to find a real life casualty because they could put their survival training into practice! They cobbled together a stretcher with some branches, and carried her to hospital. Dilys came back a short time later, found Mother had vanished and went into a complete blind panic.

All was well though, and the doctors were treating Mother nearby, but she was totally delirious.

"Must get the family back together," she rasped, lapsing in and out of consciousness.

"What's the matter Mrs Watling?" asked Mr Baticharia, our family doctor.

"Must get the family back together," she kept repeating. "Nowhere to live."

"Don't worry about it, I've got the perfect place for you," he smiled reassuringly. "Alderton Hall."

And that is how we found Alderton Hall, which became the family home for twenty-nine years.

I can recall the first time I set my eyes on the place. We drove down the driveway and there was this beautiful large building, with its bright white boarded walls. I thought it was wonderful, like a fairy palace. It was an old farm house, which had been adapted and renovated over many years; built in the 15th century, with some of the original beams in the ceiling, put there by the monks of nearby Waltham Abbey. The garden was a sprawling overgrown vision peppered with vibrant red poppies shooting up from the tall blades of grass. I took Giles round the back of the Hall for a walk through the flowers. It was just divine; three acres of garden for me to play in!

Mother, however, took one look at it and burst into tears.

"Get me out of here," she sobbed. "I can't cope with a house this big."

It was true that the place needed some work. There was only one item of furniture in the whole building; a wooden chair, which these days resides in my mother's bathroom. The beams were painted a strange brown colour, not the usual black, and it all looked rather murky and bleak. There were eight bedrooms, all completely covered in a thick layer of dust. Having had the stress of trying to find somewhere suitable, Mother now didn't want the pain of trying to make the place habitable.

"Of course you can cope," said Nanny assertively. "We'll do it together."

It turned out to be the most wonderful home we could possibly have hoped for. None of us wanted ever to leave it; and even when we'd grown up, we kept coming back.

"Oh no," said Dad with mock indignation, answering the door each time. "I thought I'd got rid of you!"

It was a big task maintaining the Hall. Rather like painting the Forth Bridge; you started at one end, and by the time you reached the other, it was time to go back to the start again. We went along to Ambrose's, the local auction house, to buy some more furniture. Obviously we had some in storage, but with a larger house we had many more rooms to fill. Despite the grand name, Alderton Hall was not smart at all. It had a kind of tatty elegance to it.

With a house that size, inevitably we needed some help with the cleaning and gardening. There was an estate at the side of the Hall call the Devdon Estate, and our cleaner Marge lived there with her husband and two kids. She worked for us a few days a week, but was sadly quite light-fingered. Sometimes I would be searching madly through my wardrobe for a top I wanted to wear, and then give up, thinking it was in the wash, only to see her daughter wearing the said top in the local high street the next day.

Things came to a head over a large chest of drawers, which was situated on the landing just outside my room. One morning I went outside and it had vanished. I was puzzled; it was a heavy piece of furniture, it couldn't have just gone. I went back into my room and gazed out of the window. There, on the path below, was Marge, with her son, carrying the drawers out of the house and away down the drive. I pulled the window open in an instant.

"What on earth are you doing?!" I bellowed down at the duo.

"What do you mean?" she called back, innocently.

"With the chest of drawers?" I continued. "What are you doing with it?"

"Oh," she said playing dumb. "I thought you didn't need it any more."

There she was nicking our furniture, caught in the act, and she still didn't put her hands up. In the end we had to get rid of her, which was a shame, because pilfering aside, she was a rather pleasant lady.

Another lovely lady from my childhood was Elsie from down the end of the lane who used to be our babysitter. Every time she came to look after us she would bring us all a Fry's Five Boys chocolate bar. You can't buy them now, but they used to have five boys' heads made from chocolate along the bar, and we loved them. Elsie and Nanny were the best of friends, and then we took on Elsie's husband Dick as our gardener. He was a bit old to deal with three acres, but he became like one of the family, so we kept him on. Dick was very good at dealing with the more rural problems one faces in the country; he could clear a nest of adders with a pitchfork, or vanquish a nest of rats and so on. He was also a great believer in what I call the "old ways" and folklore. Mother had a big wart on her neck at one point, which she became terribly conscious of. Dick told her not to go to the doctors, but to marinate a steak, rest the steak on the wart for a while, then let him bury the steak in the garden.

"As that steak rots away," he said knowingly, "so will your wart."

We all thought he was a bit mad, I mean you can't cure a wart with a steak, but Mummy did it all the same. And it worked. Within a week her wart had completely disappeared!

We were always surrounded by all sorts of different characters at the Hall. There was the family with their various friends and partners stopping over, and an assortment of different lodgers we took in, much like when we were in Epping. One guy even ran his own secondhand car business from our front drive. Daddy didn't complain at all, because he didn't think he was doing anyone any harm. Then there was Myra, who came to live with us and brought along her little white poodle, Fudge. He was a cheery little soul, but had terrible halitosis, so we didn't like to get too close.

We used to have wonderful parties at the Hall, and I remember there being one for Dilys's birthday one year. Everybody was dressed up and dancing, and having a wonderful time, and I set my eyes upon this beautiful blue-eyed boy sat on the stairs. I wasn't terribly old, and was quite shy, but we sat and chatted for a while. Then he kissed me: my first ever kiss. By strange coincidence of how life runs, the boy in question was one Michael Craze whom I would later take over from in *Doctor Who*, and with whom I attended many conventions. Who was to know?

I got my first boyfriend when I was about sixteen years old, whilst I was at Brayside School. He was a handsome boy called John, and he went to a school up the road. He used to wait outside for me on his moped and watch me come out. One day we got chatting, and he asked if I would like to go round to his house for tea. I said that was a lovely idea, and he said he'd borrow his mother's car and pick me up that evening. John had only ever seen me in my school uniform, and was quite shocked when I came to the front door in my casual clothes. It was the days of white pop socks under the knees, little flat shoes and miniskirts. His face dropped at this vision, because I looked about ten years old! He later told me that I looked like "jailbait"!

We started to go out with each other seriously. He was a couple of years older than me, but that didn't seem to matter and we were together for a long time. However, I started to get TV work, and meet new people, and he became quite jealous of the circles I was beginning to move in. We were on and off so many times it was hard to keep track of; and when we were together it was a very tempestuous affair, and we would sometimes come to physical blows with each other.

For a while he lived in the flat above my boutique, The Pink Clock. By this point the television work had picked up again, and I was seeing less and less of him.

"Come over to the flat," he said one day, on the phone. "I want to see you."

The flat had communicating doors that ran right the way through. So as you got to one door, it was possible to lock it behind you. I entered the flat, and he locked the front door behind me, then we went through the sitting room and he did the same. I could tell I was in trouble. Eventually we came to a halt, and he produced a pump gun I had given him as a Christmas present a few years previously, and pointed it at me. My blood ran cold. He had totally lost it.

"What are you doing John?" I asked calmly.

"I can't take much more," his voice quivered. "This is it."

"What is 'it'?"

Slowly he turned the gun round on himself, and pulled my finger over the trigger, trying to make me fire it.

"No!" I yelled, wrenching myself free.

Then he collapsed to the floor, sobbing uncontrollably.

"Listen," I said, crouching next to him. "You need help John. We'll get you help, professional help; there's something terribly wrong with you."

He was an academic guy, with a PhD and a top scientific job in a research laboratory. To see that he had just crumbled to this was awful. He did get help, thankfully, but we were no longer a couple.

A few years ago we met again at a funeral.

"You're looking very well," he smiled.

"Thank you," I replied politely.

Conversation moved along, and I asked if he had ever married.

"No," he said, looking straight back at me. "There was only ever one person for me."

And with that he turned and walked away, and I haven't seen him since.

~

Given the great age of Alderton Hall, it's inevitable that there are many ghost stories attached to it. I know a lot of people don't believe in such things, but I am a very firm believer and have had many supernatural experiences in my life. There were several ghosts at the hall, and not all of them friendly. In fact we had some very nasty poltergeist activity during our time there.

On one occasion I promised to lend Nicky, my younger sister, a dress for a party she was going to. I had seen it hung up in my wardrobe the night before, so she ran up the stairs to fetch it. Nicky pulled open the doors, and there, still on the hanger, was this beautiful green frock absolutely torn to shreds. She rushed up to me in tears, shredded frock in hand. It was an horrific sight; something so violent had literally sliced it to pieces. I told Nicky that it was probably the wind; however, she insisted that the window wasn't open.

On another evening I was babysitting Nicky, and we went to bed together in a large oak four-poster bed. We awoke in the night and everything on the bedside table was swept off and smashed across the floor. I told her not to worry, hugged her close and tried to get back to sleep. When morning came the bed had moved away from the wall by a good three feet. How could there be a rational explanation for that?

There were many, many more instances of such spooky goings-on, including a cavalier who used to be spotted on our drive; but Father would always play these things down, probably because he didn't want to alarm us. I know he used to laugh at Mum because she would lock the bedroom door to stop the ghost who walked the landing from coming into her room when he was away on tour.

"He's a ghost, Pat," he chided. "I hardly think a locked door is going to stop him!"

The haunting of Alderton Hall was picked up by many newspapers and magazines, and for a while we used to get parties of ghost hunters coming to visit to see if they could make contact with the other side. One such party was made up of a group of Americans, and we split the group into two; Dilys took one party round and I looked after the other. It was late at night, and the Hall was dimly lit by all the lamps, which in itself lent a very spooky atmosphere. I had just taken my party into the most haunted room in the building, which happened to be my bedroom, when the lights rapidly flickered on and off, before plunging us into total darkness. The screams were deafening! There was a mass of arms and legs pushing past and tumbling down the stairs to get out, running in abject terror. What had caused this sinister occurrence?

Giles. My little brother had decided it would be funny to go downstairs to the fuse box, and play a little game on us all. We saw the humorous side to it… eventually!

Chapter Two

It was always rather assumed by my teachers that I would become an actress. To me, it was a very normal thing to do. Whereas other children would wave off their daddy to the office each morning, mine would go to the studio. I only realised this differed from the norm one day when I was sat in class and felt a tap on my back.

"Here, can I have your dad's autograph?" asked the girl behind me.

I was bemused.

"What's that?"

"Well," she explained. "He writes his name down on a piece of paper."

I was none the wiser.

"What for?"

"Because he's famous!"

I couldn't for the life of me comprehend why she wanted my father to write his name on a piece of paper.

My first taste of the acting life came when I was about three. Daddy was making a film, and the director needed two children to stand and eat ice cream in front of a doorway.

"I've got two girls you can have," offered Father proudly.

I think that makes him my first agent! Dilys and myself were duly packed off to the set, and I was really excited. I was going to spend all day eating ice cream, which is a dream for any three-year-old. What I had anticipated as paradise soon turned into a complete nightmare, as we shot take after take, which meant having to eat ice cream after ice cream, until I began to feel nauseous. Dil loved every minute of it, and kept wolfing them down *ad nauseum*, but I had reached my limit and threw up. No more ice cream for me! To this day I'm still not very keen.

My stage debut came around in a similarly serendipitous way. We were on our family holiday to Frinton-on-Sea, larking about on the beach, when Peter Hoar, who ran Frinton Theatre, came along to say hello to Daddy. It turned out they were putting on a production of *Roar Like a Dove* for their summer season, and the girl they'd cast could no longer do it. Would it be possible for me to take on the role? Father had a quick think, and agreed, so in I went to rehearse for five days, before making the first of many appearances at Frinton Summer Theatre. I still have the original letter from the Essex Education Committee granting me permission to take part; as a minor I needed a special licence to take part in any production, be it on film or stage. The education officer rather sternly asserts that the licence is granted because the engagement is during the school holidays, and that any future application during term time would be dependent on an improvement in my school work, concluding that I "could not afford to have (my) attention further distracted by taking part in entertainment."

I recall the leading man in the production, Mike Johnston, was rather dishy; and I cultivated quite a major crush, as one does when one is a child. I can still see my entrance onto the stage even now at Frinton Theatre; I came in downstage right and had to leaf through a telephone directory, looking up somebody's number. My Uncle Dennis was very proud that I went straight to the 'S' section to look the name up, which as it began with an 'S' seemed very natural to me. Adults could be such strange people.

The local bookmaker, Ted, took a shine to me during the run. Not in a sinister way; nowadays I think we are liable to put labels all over the place which we didn't in those days. I was only twelve, so he asked my parents' permission to take me out to dinner one evening. They had no problem with it, so he took me out for a meal and bought me a dozen red roses. He was a nice man and came to see me every day at the theatre; he saw that play over and over. Little did I know I would still be associated with the theatre over fifty years on!

My major breakthrough role as a child was in the ITC series *The Invisible Man*, playing Sally Brady, the niece of the epnoymous hero. My godfather rang my father up one day and said:

"They're doing a TV version of *The Invisible Man* by H.G. Wells, and they're casting the young niece. I think you should send Debs up for it."

Mummy and Daddy were not too sure whether it would be wise to let me take on the part. They knew how unstable the acting world could be, but on the other hand how rewarding. Would it be worth sacrificing my education to send me out into the big wide world of work so early on? Father later told me that he felt he never truly knew if they had made the right decision. The auditions for *The Invisible Man* were held at Elstree Studios, and my mother came along with me as my chaperone. The place was simply breathtaking; the carpets were so rich and deep that my feet literally just sank into them. We were taken into a room where a well-dressed man, who was sat welcomingly behind a large desk, introduced himself as Ralph Smart, the producer.

"Would you like to be Sally?" he asked, smiling.

"OK," said I, with all the non-committal enthusiasm of a ten-year-old.

The man was not put off by this.

"Right, well I'd like you to read the script."

I eyed him up and down.

"Read?" I asked.

"Yes dear, read," smiled Mother.

I looked at her, then back at Ralph.

"I can't read," I replied curtly.

Mother had had enough of this attitude and gave me a sharp kick under the desk.

"Of course you can read," she grinned through firmly gritted teeth.

Despite such auspicious beginnings, I was chosen to become Sally, and I note from my original contract (which I still have) that Father negotiated me an increase from the original £25 per episode I was offered to a mighty £35 per show. The major thrill for me, however, was when I realised I was going to get the chance to have my own make-up artist to do my make-up for me, like a real movie actress. Marvellous! The lovely make-up man said:

"Sit back in the chair, close your eyes and I'll begin".

I began to imagine all the extensive preparations that were taking place, and how much of a glamorous Hollywood star I would look. Wrong. I opened my eyes and was devastated; instead of luscious lips and accentuated eyes, I had a splattering of freckles all over my nose and cheeks. So much for glamorous!

Glamorous was a word which could be readily attributed to my co-star and onscreen mother, Lisa Danielle. She was a stunning looking lady, and still is, as I found when we recently met up for a DVD commentary. I can also remember quite clearly the scandal surrounding Tim Turner being sacked from his part as the Invisible Man. He got terribly grand and demanded, of all things, a stand-in. Such demands were not tolerated and he was sent packing. Clumsiness was altogether less punishable, otherwise I would have been in some serious trouble. The visual effects guys used to toil for hours on end elaborately setting bits of string and wire to make the "invisible" movements on set, such as cups lifting, doors opening and so on. Being young and full of enthusiasm, I would be stood watching with amazement off set, and then when I was called into position would go bounding on, carefree, straight into the wires, inadvertently ruining their careful preparations, and getting myself completely tangled up and red-faced with embarrassment.

It was whilst filming *The Invisible Man* that I was "headhunted" for the first time. *William Tell* was being shot in the studio next door, and they were on the lookout for a girl of my age to make a small appearance as a child carried off by the villain. It was only a cameo, but they specifically requested me, and so off I popped into the neighbouring studio to record my scene. I think that it actually ended up being broadcast before *The Invisible Man*, so whilst *Invisible* was my first proper recorded television, *William Tell* was the first to go out.

Even as a nine-year-old, I quickly cottoned on that one of the benefits to filming was that it would mean getting time off school. Unfortunately, as is still the case, child actors do not get away with avoiding doing the work: you get given a tutor. I had three hours a day put aside to spend with my tutor to prevent getting behind with my education, and I hated it. All the prop boys knew I hated it too, and would help to hide me from my tutor, by putting me behind crates or secreting me behind unused scenery. I was terrible, and put such a strain on the poor women sent to teach me; I got through three in a year, with two of them leaving with nervous breakdowns.

My next big acting role on television was in a sitcom called *A Life Of Bliss*, which was transmitted live from the BBC's Riverside Studios. We would have a week's rehearsal, then it would go out on the Saturday evening. The lead in *Bliss* was a man who had been very instrumental in getting my parents together in the first place, George Cole, and I was playing his niece. It was whilst appearing in this that I first saw an actor lose their nerve completely. As the show was broadcast live there was no question of being able to stop or go back; what you did went straight out, much like theatre. The titles would be cued in studio and then the floor manager would count us in ready for our first shot. One day Isabel Dean, the actress playing my mother, began to shake and shriek. Then she began to scream.

"I can't do it!" she yelped.

"10, 9, 8..." counted in the floor manager.

"I can't, I can't!" she wailed, slapping her hand on the table.

"...7, 6," he continued, then started making the gestures for five, down to one.

And on cue, as if there had never been a problem, she went straight into the scene and was fine for the whole episode. She'd got her nerve back. Children feel no such fear. Seeing things, as one does as a child, from a more simplistic point of view, I couldn't understand what the silly woman was doing and was unmoved by the whole event. Losing nerve is a commonplace thing in acting. Not so much now television is recorded and edited, but most definitely in the theatre, where an actor will suddenly go blank, have no concept of what their next line is or even sometimes which play they're in. This was the first, but by no means the last time I would encounter the phenomenon.

Having completed *A Life Of Bliss* and *Roar Like a Dove* very close to each other, I then began to wonder whether I really wanted to pursue a career as an actor. What other options were available? For about two weeks I became resolved not to follow the rest of the family into showbusiness, but to do something more academic, and settled on becoming a dentist. When you're as short as I am (five foot for the record), the first thing you notice about a person when you meet them is their teeth, because you are on that level, so dentistry held a great appeal. That was until I realised quite how many exams I'd have to pass, and then I dropped the thought completely from my mind.

I was attending Bayside School for Girls whilst making *A Life Of Bliss*, and I actually got a harder time off my teachers than I did from my fellow pupils. You would expect other children to take against my success, but it was the teachers who were jealous and thought I was being terribly grand doing the acting work. Not that it stopped them from asking my father to open their school fêtes and give speeches. In particular I remember one instance where I had been in the studio and had forgotten to do my French homework. This was totally out of character because I would always make sure I did any school work, but on this occasion I hadn't remembered.

"Where's your homework?" barked the French teacher.

"I'm terribly sorry, but I forgot it," I said.

"Don't give me that," she sneered.

"It's true," I insisted.

"Who do you think you are?" she berated, towering over me. "You go off and do your TV work, but academically you are useless. And you always will be. Now do the work and bring it to me first thing tomorrow. Understand me?"

The notable exception to this kind of nastiness was my science teacher, who was very enthusiastic and took the time to try and encourage me. Dissecting things and playing around with Bunsen burners wasn't something I naturally gravitated towards, but with her support I actually passed my mock 'O' level, and was so proud. I used to work harder for her because she made the effort with me. I used to enjoy art, music, dance and sport. Sport was brilliant, and I was actually captain of several teams like hockey, tennis and netball. I was five foot nothing and all the other girls were towering above me, but I was still sports captain.

But on the whole I was never very keen on school, so when the opportunity arose to leave, I grabbed it with both hands. As a fully formed teenager, I felt my own person, and I politely pushed aside requests from my teachers to stay on and complete my 'A' levels; I couldn't see the point. Instead I enrolled at stage school, and picked the Italia Conti, where my father had trained. My parents were both away opening a television station in Australia, so I was acting as a kind of surrogate mother figure at home to Nan, Nicky and Giles. Nan was quite merrily going potty and wandering the streets, Giles was running away from boarding school on a daily basis; thank goodness Nicky was well behaved.

On top of this, my new stage school endeavour was starting to look bleak. Instead of actively promoting individuality, they seemed hell bent on creating a series of clones off a production line: all-singing, all-dancing entertainment machines devoid of any creativity whatsoever. I spoke to Father about my dismay at the training I was being given, and he concurred that things had changed greatly since his time there. It became readily apparent that I would have to say goodbye to Italia Conti, and begin to make my own way in the big wide world. So I quit, and got myself an agent, Jimmy Vickers, who was also Daddy's agent, and set about forging a career as an actress.

My first post drama school engagement had more than a touch of nepotism about it. *Monique* was a play being put on by my father and a man called Henry Sherwood, and they cast me as the young girl next door. We opened at the Leeds Grand Theatre, and toured for a while, before it was decided that we would go into the West End, to the Savoy Theatre. Henry Sherwood's father, who was a great man of the theatre, was slightly worried about having me in the cast when we moved into the West End because it was my first major job and he didn't think I would cope with it. So they rehearsed and rehearsed and rehearsed me, and I did get better, but it was made very clear that if I hadn't then I would have been out. It wasn't a remarkable play, but I enjoyed it, and it was great experience. It was a real family affair too, as Mother was acting as my chaperone once more, and brought Nicky and Giles along to stop in digs with us.

❧

Winning the leading role in *The Wednesday Play* was a very prestigious thing. I played the title role in *Alice* and the script was written by Dennis Potter. People often ask me what it was like to work with Dennis, but in all honesty I didn't get the chance to see him very much. He was a shy, introverted man, and would just come along to rehearsals, stand and watch, but say nothing. In fact I felt there was quite a lot of his shyness reflected in the character of Lewis Carroll in this piece. The play fused together the real-life story of Lewis Carroll (Mr Dodgson) and his association with Alice Liddell, and some recreations of sections of *Alice's Adventures in Wonderland*. Unlike other productions which just feature Alice going down the hole to meet the White Rabbit and so on, the main focus of this was the relationship between the real Alice and Mr Dodgson. Although never explicity stated, it is clear that Mr Dodgson is in love with this underage girl, something which was very sensitively handled by Potter.

The character I was playing was only meant to be twelve years old, whereas in reality I was by this point a well-developed seventeen-year-old, meaning that I had to be strapped very firmly to hold my breasts down and appear more flat-chested. That, combined with the very tight period corsets, led on more than one occasion to my nearly passing out cold. I was always very thankful to reach the end of the day and be set free again!

As was the norm in those days, we did all the location filming before the studio work. For *Alice* we did the bulk of this around a college in Oxford, and then on the river. This was my first job without a chaperone; up until the age of seventeen it was always necessary for me to be accompanied by an adult. As a result I had a whale of a time being put up in a very posh hotel with a room to myself, and felt quite the independent young adult. It was also therefore the first role I had taken on where my parents hadn't vetted the script. It had some very strong adult themes, but as we were all actors there was no debate about doing it; you just get on and play it.

My agent at the time was Jimmy Vickers, but Mary Madir had asked if she could represent me instead. She represented my sister Dilys, and I was not very keen on having the same agent as I didn't think it would be beneficial. Mary took it upon herself to put my name on her books, and there was an almighty row when I was given the part of Alice as to which agent would get the commission. I had never had any intention of leaving Jimmy; Mary had just assumed I would move to her agency. Mary's husband, Laurie, was a singing teacher. He'd taught Julie Andrews, and my sister, so when I later came to do *The Wizard of Oz*, I took him on as my teacher too; I didn't mind sharing a singing teacher with Dil, but not an agent!

There was one major problem I encountered on location for *Alice*, and that was that I was called upon to laugh. That might not sound like a big challenge to overcome, but I had never previously been called upon to laugh on cue. We came to the take, and the moment arrived where I had to giggle hysterically, and I just stopped. I couldn't do it.

"I can't do it, I'm sorry," I said, shaking my head.

"Of course you can, just laugh!" said the director.

"No," I frowned. "I can't do it to order like that!"

So they had to teach me to "laugh". The director went through it in a very technical way; breathing in, then pushing the air out in a particular way. I did it, but I cringe terribly now when I hear it, because it sounds so fake and forced. It's awful.

The cast were all very friendly and professional, with the exception of Tessa Wyatt, who played my sister. She was very resentful of not being the lead, and made it very uncomfortable to share scenes. She wasn't outright hostile, but she was sarcastic and unpleasant the whole time. I met her many years later, however, and we were fine together. George Baker played Lewis Carroll, and he was a delight. We shared many scenes together and became quite close. In those days it was the etiquette to call your leading actor "sir", so I naturally called him sir during rehearsals.

"Debbie," he said suddenly, one day. "Will you please stop calling me sir! It's George!"

From then on, George it was! I met him a few years back when they did a screening of *Alice* at the National Film

Theatre. We hadn't seen each other since the day we finished filming. He'd got a bit greyer and a bit fuller round the waist.

"How old were you when we did *Alice*?" he asked, eyebrow raised quizzically.

"About eighteen I think," I replied.

"Are you sure?" he said, looking me up and down.

"Definitely," I smiled.

George was never the most demonstrative of fellows.

"You're looking terribly well," he said indignantly.

One of the great joys of doing *The Wednesday Play* was that I was given the front cover of *Radio Times*. It's still a big deal today, but back then it was huge. I had no idea it was going to happen either; I recall the photo session by the river bank in Oxford for the production, but had no knowledge that one of the pictures would be used for *Radio Times*. I was the first family member to get the cover shot, and Mummy and Daddy were very proud of me. I think Giles got one later on when the cast of *Bread* were featured, but I'm the only one to manage it solo! I still have a framed copy at home.

This Man Craig was a television series shot in Glasgow, starring John Cairney, and I was invited to appear in an episode. Cairney was a deeply unpleasant character. It was 1966, and I was a very shy young thing, on my own, very far from home. Although I was eighteen, I was once again cast younger, this time playing a schoolgirl. The programme was a smash hit, and Cairney was adored in Glasgow, so I was slightly apprehensive entering rehearsal. However, Cairney proved to be attentive. Very attentive. So much so that on one occasion, against my better judgement, I agreed to visit his home where he became very forceful in his affections. Not a happy memory.

A more pleasant recollection from the filming, and quite a strange one, came one day in the canteen. One of the extras playing a schoolgirl was sat lunching with me when, quite out of the blue, a voice popped into my head. I don't why or from where, but it kept telling me that the girl needed to phone her mother. I can't claim to be a great psychic, but I have been told that I am in touch with my more spiritual side. At this moment I was just as sceptical as most, and wary as to how I could broach the subject.

"Have you phoned your mother recently?" I asked, as nonchalant as possible.

"No, I haven't," she replied, finishing another mouthful. "Why?"

"I suggest you do," I replied ashen-faced.

"I don't understand!"

"Neither do I, I just have a voice telling me," I started, beginning to sound a little outlandish. "Please just phone her right away."

As strange as I was seeming, she complied and vanished off to make the call. A few minutes later she returned, somewhat more pale-faced.

"How did you know?" she asked in amazement.

"What is it?"

"Mum's been trying to get in touch for days and couldn't get hold of me," she started. "Dad's been taken seriously ill and I need to get back there."

How could I have known? The poor girl obviously thought I was completely barking, but thank goodness I spoke out!

A year after *Alice*, I was cast in another *Wednesday Play*, *Calf Love*. My sister was played by Isobel Black, who was a very gentle girl and we went on to work together again not so long after in an episode of the police crime drama series *No Hiding Place*, which was huge at the time. Simon Ward was playing the lead role in *Calf Love*, and his character swayed between fancying the two sisters. He's always ribbed me that I was his first screen kiss, but having recently reviewed the show, I can tell him that he is very much mistaken. We have a fumble under the pear tree, but it's Isobel who gets all the action. As is often the case with my roles, I'm just a big tease!

Warren Mitchell played my father, and he was quite a stickler. Rehearsals were a very formal affair in those days: the ladies would never be allowed to wear jeans, and you had to be very respectful in how you addressed the senior members of the cast. One day I arrived in a skirt and top which didn't quite match, and I caught Warren looking at me disdainfully across the room. We took a quick tea break, and he called me over to one side.

"Look, this simply won't do," he said. "You have to dress properly for rehearsals, do you understand?"

He wasn't being a tyrant as such, more a very stern father. I received a similar telling-off when I wore a trouser suit a few days later. It seemed jeans were an abomination, but trousers for girls were also a no-no!

We had three weeks to rehearse the play because it was so complicated, then we shot it over a full day in studio at Television Centre, in order. There were a few pre-filmed inserts which were played in, but several breaks would be factored in to allow for costume changes, and different wigs to be fitted. I had several for this one, which had to be hired in from a specialist shop in London. The studio session would be something like nine in the morning to seven at night, and it had to be finished on the dot. To go over your allotted time would incur a terrible cost.

There was one sequence set during a party where we had to perform an elaborate formal dance. I had loved ballet and Greek dance lessons when I was a child, then jazz and modern later on; but I was never really a dancer, more a mover. This was hampered even further when I developed a knee injury, meaning I had to stop dancing altogether. It used to pop out when I moved too vigorously, something which cost me a role in the Twiggy film *The Boyfriend*. I made it right the way down to the last few to play her friend, and my knee shot out, so they wouldn't touch me.

Another missed opportunity came in 1967 when I was cast as Jim Dale's girlfriend in a sitcom called *Mr Misfit*. I had to play the sexy glamorous sort of girl, and I recall one scene where I had to very elegantly paint my toenails and look provocatively at him. They knew I wasn't right, and so did I. In the end they phoned up my agent and said they had miscast me. The problem was that I looked too young. In 1967 I was nineteen years old, but looked much younger, so it didn't work pairing the two of us up on screen. It wasn't my fault, but it meant I didn't get to do it. Jim was great to work with, even though I only got to spend three days with him. Despite being a major star at the time with the *Carry On* films he was appearing in, he was very down to earth with a wonderful sense of humour. Still, the whole episode was an experience, and as an actor you learn to deal with these things.

Chapter Three

There has never been, and never will be, any confusion in my mind as to how I came to be cast as Victoria Waterfield in *Doctor Who*. Despite what certain authors may have written to the contrary, it is very clear to me how I became involved in the series. I initially went into the production office for a meeting with the producer, Innes Lloyd. Not a specific audition for a part (I certainly didn't go up for the part of Polly as some people would have you believe), more a general chat about joining the show. Innes was very much of the opinion that I should take some time to "learn my craft" as he put it, and come back in a year or so. Which of course I did, appearing in the meantime in various plays and television productions. Innes knew how intense the workload could be on *Who*, so he was quite right in asking me to get some more working experience before taking it on.

So in early 1967, back I went to Innes's office to talk about becoming the new companion. We had a chat, I didn't even have to read a script, and was offered the part there and then. As simple as that! For something which was to play such a great role in my life, and indeed still does to this day, I must confess that I knew very little about *Doctor Who* itself. I had, of course, seen some episodes. In fact I can clearly remember seeing the first episode with William Hartnell as the Doctor, but other than that I hadn't taken much notice. Not because I has anything against the show, more that I was usually working; the only programme we watched with any regularity was *The Power Game*, and once again that was only to see Dad!

I was introduced to Patrick Troughton and Frazer Hines at a party held in a grand house by the River Thames. There were press galore and I remember being quite startled by the intense media interest. Patrick became a truly great friend to me. We used to go to tea together, sometimes with his first wife, then later with his second wife… he was a great lover of ladies! And ladies adored him too. He had a kind of sexual appeal, a magnetism that was quite indescribable. I mean he wasn't tall or muscular, but he just had ladies falling at his feet all the time. I suppose the three of us were custom-picked to perform our different roles; Pat as the father figure, me for the dads, Frazer for the girls. And boy did Frazer like that! Talk about typecasting! There was a different girl every other story with Frazer. Pamela Franklyn, Susan George… He always had an eye for the girls. Still does in fact!

My first story was a seven-part epic entitled *The Evil of the Daleks*, and I've lost count of the number of photos I've signed that were taken during its making. Literally hundreds of different shots of me walking round the garden in that great flowing Victorian dress, so wonderfully designed by Sandra Reid. I really loved that frock and wish I'd kept it now! It was crinoline, with lots of different layers and petticoats and the bones round it to help it keep its shape. Walking in it was less easy, although one got used to that, and I ended up gliding around just like those dreaded Daleks.

Of course, the long flowing skirts of the sweet Victorian Miss were not to last. From *Tomb of the Cybermen* onwards, with a steady progression, they began to get shorter and shorter, and by the time we reached *Fury from the Deep* I was virtually in a pelmet. It was ridiculous! This didn't go unnoticed by either myself or my co-stars, and we conspired to mention it on screen. As the Doctor, Jamie and Victoria prepare to enter the Cybermen's tomb, she holds back and the Doctor tells her what a pretty dress she is wearing.

"Don't you think it's a bit…" falters Victoria.

"Short? No, I shouldn't worry. Look at Jamie's!" chirps the Doctor.

That was typical of the cheeky humour we had, that we managed to slip into the series at any given opportunity. In fact Pat used to make up outrageously bad jokes so that the directors would allow him to put in less outrageous ones which were the ones he really wanted to put in anyway in the first place!

꩜

The guest actors on my first story were quite phenomenal when I look back: Windsor Davies, Marius Goring and the like. I got on particularly well with Brigit Forsyth, who was playing Ruth Maxtible. She was debating whether or not to marry her fiancé at the time, and we discussed it a lot during breaks in rehearsal. I told her to follow her gut instinct and if she was questioning it, then he wasn't completely right for her. She was a lovely girl and we spent a lot of time together during that story. Years later Windsor Davies played Baron Hardup to my Cinderella at the Theatre Royal, Nottingham. He had a great sense of humour and that wonderful gruff Welsh tone to his voice. Also in *The Evil of the Daleks*, but better known to *Who* fans as an Ice Warrior, was Sonny Caldinez. A huge, great man who became terribly protective of me. He protected Victoria on screen and extended that to me in rehearsal. It was like having my own bodyguard; he even escorted me to the car when I went home! I met him again five years ago and he hadn't changed a bit, still massive and warm, and protective.

My first day of filming took place at a grand old house in Harrow, owned by Gilbert of Gilbert and Sullivan fame. I was nervous, as one always is on such occasions, but it's so hard to describe quite how it felt when one's co-stars were these… well Daleks! Tin things with bumps all over them and plungers; it's quite bizarre. I thought "Well here we go Watling, you've got to look really terrified." Quite simply if I didn't look terrified, then the audience wouldn't think they were scary! The first shot was a long corridor with a Dalek marching me down to my cell and it looked quite funny because you couldn't see either of our feet; I glided along and the line of my skirt mirrored that of the Dalek skirts, albeit not wooden and without the blue spots!

Then of course came the legendary scene with Frazer. Jamie, being the noble young Scot that he was, was on a mission to rescue Victoria. Derek Martinus was the director on this story, and everything was set for the take, which went something like this:

"Miss Victoria, are you all right?" asked Jamie.

"Well, I don't know… There are these terrible creatures… We ought to get out of here!"

"Yes Victoria, quick, quick! Up your passage!"

And we stopped. I looked at Frazer, my nineteen-year-old face starting to redden with embarrassment.

"He can't say that!!!" I said.

And we both started to laugh. Derek, who didn't have much of a sense of humour, was nonplussed.

"Why can't you say it?"

Explaining it to him made it worse for us both. We literally fell about laughing, and he just didn't get it!

Unfortunately, the director for my next serial was also something of a character. Morris Barry was the appointed director of *The Tomb of the Cybermen*, and was what I like to call "of the old school". He had a music stand fixed in place and used to tap it with a baton. This music stand sadly travelled with him from the rehearsal room to the studio, and became a symbol of much mirth amongst the team. The worst was yet to come. We arrived at the studio with the sets all in place, cameras ready to roll, and there was a tap of the baton.

"The set's wrong," announced Morris gravely.

The prop guys were bemused.

"I want it moved four inches to the left," he decreed.

"Well, why don't we just move the cameras?" offered a sane member of the production team.

"No," said Morris, indignantly. "We don't move my cameras."

So he made them move the whole set, *the whole set*, a mere *four inches* to the left. It took forever to do, and did not make for a very harmonious atmosphere! I did get my own back on Morris a few years later. In the early nineties I was attending a convention called Blue Box in Bournemouth and it was suggested that I should interview, which I thought would make a nice change. The panel was made up of my dad, Victor Pemberton and Morris. Vic and Dad sent me up something rotten, as they often did, but Morris was completely flummoxed when questioned and kept saying he'd have to think about it and come back to me later. Ha! I'd got him, on stage in front of all those people. I never manage to stay on top for long in a panel when paired up with the likes of Vic. Dad sent the place into uproarious laughter when he looked at me and said:

"So did Victoria get a lot of sex?"

Cue red face stage left!

&

I really liked the Cybermen as monsters. One gets asked often to pick a favourite monster, and I think that the Cybermen take some beating. I worked with all the classic monsters, but they were the eeriest, because they looked like a sort of person, but an altered one. Of course, the chaps inside the costumes were less scary. Big Reg Whitehead was a Cyberman in this adventure, then later a Yeti, and he took me out on a date during filming. Only once, but what a picture we made. Reg, a well-built six foot five inches, me a petite five foot nothing! We had our dinner and then he asked me to dance. Well, I could hardly refuse. People watched in amazement as we tried to dance our way round. In the end Reg picked me up and swung me round instead, earning an impromptu round of applause from our fellow diners!

Whilst we are on the subject of amorous liaisons, my mind is cast over another of my co-stars, Bernard Holley. Not that I liaised with him in any way, but I do remember having an almighty crush on him at the time.

I watched *Tomb* recently and I do wonder how we got away with some of the stuff we recorded. The Cyberman who has goo spurting from his chest and things like that is actually quite scary. As was the sequence where they awoke from their tombs and broke free – even if it was only clingfilm. In many ways the special effects were more important than the actors on a studio day. We'd had all week to rehearse our lines, so we had to stand back and wait for the effects to be prepared. I was fascinated by it all, and the boys really did work miracles for next to no money at all. In the next story we had terrible problems with Wolfe Morris's character; he was the chief monk and had to die at the end of the serial. The effects team made a cast of his face, and then poured acid on it until it eroded to a skull layer. We watched them do it on the studio floor and agreed that they just couldn't do it. It was a step too far and we'd get too many complaining letters, as well as frightening the children to death!

Another thing which comes back to me when thinking about *Tomb* is a great scene that Pat and I got to share. It's one which I get asked about a lot by fans, where Victoria is sat on guard by the tomb entrance. She is meant to have woken the Doctor up for his turn at watch duty, but hasn't because she thinks that, as an old man, he needs his sleep! Of course he wakes up, and the two of them have a very tender discussion about missing their families. It's a very quiet little scene, but a nice character piece, and I'm very proud of it. I used to drive to the studio when we were recording, but I remember I had terrible 'flu the day we recorded this episode, so a car was sent for me. We made it all the way through the scene, then just at the last moment I fluffed terribly. Unfortunately, the scene ran straight on and there was no way to just cut in and pick it up, so we had to go again straight from the top. I didn't think I would make it through, I was so lethargic and spaced out. Maybe that's how it worked! Recording could be terribly frenetic because, although we weren't being broadcast live, we shot it as though we were, with as few breaks as possible, which meant a lot of very speedy movement from set to set. We had to change costumes on the run, all the time making sure we kept as quiet as church mice because other scenes were still being recorded, and panicking in case we didn't make our cue on time. It was terribly basic, but totally thrilling!

I hold the next story in great affection for a number of reasons. With *The Abominable Snowmen* we had the great glamour of location filming up in Snowdonia in north Wales, and the whole team were encamped in a motel a little way down the road from where we were shooting. The director on this one was Gerald Blake, and he was a wonderful man with a tremendous sense of humour. I remember one shot in particular where Frazer and I were running down a hill away from the Yeti. Now the hill was very steep and the Yeti costumes very cumbersome, and the poor Yeti slipped, rolled, and began to gather momentum, until it shot straight past us like a speeding fur ball. When it reached the bottom a small voice could be heard squealing to be let out. I cannot remain entirely aloof at this point as I too managed to lose my footing running down that hill, and remarkably there still exists an outtake where I fall out of shot with a small shriek!

We used to get the scripts a few weeks in advance of shooting, and I recall taking *Snowmen* home to read. I was leafing through it and I thought that Dad would be good for the part of Professor Travers. He might be a bit young for it, but with some make-up and a beard, he'd be ideal. So I rang Innes. He loved the idea and told me to ask him. I put the phone down and went running into the living room where Dad was reading the paper.

"There's a great part for you in *Doctor Who*," I said full of enthusiasm.

"What?" replied Father, devoid of any excitement.

"He's an explorer called Professor Travers. It's great, we could work together!" I continued, unabashed.

"I'll think about it," he said without even looking up from his paper.

I couldn't believe it! Here was our big chance to work together. I worked on him over the next week, and he eventually agreed to do it. I suppose in some ways he was reluctant to do it because *Doctor Who* was very much perceived as being a kid's show, whereas he was known for his roles in evening adult drama. It wasn't that he thought it beneath him, but six weeks, plus any location filming, is a very large commitment and I think he was unsure about doing it. Of course it became a legendary joke, as Dad would often say, "You're the only child of mine who actually got me a job!"

So Dad was welcomed into our *Who* family, as were all the guest actors on the show. He fitted in straight away, and Frazer adored him. They were like Pinky and Perky: we couldn't separate them! Pat slightly took two steps back to begin with, and I don't know why, but the three of them quite contentedly ganged up on me in the end. Travers proved such a hit with the viewers that Innes decided to get the character brought back a few months later, and approached Dad about it. Well, he'd had such fun making *The Abominable Snowmen* that he leapt at it. There's some wonderful colour footage that Gerry took during filming in Snowdonia which brings back so many memories. Dad always had a fag on the go between takes and he, Frazer and Pat used to warm up with brandy out of sight of the director. I remember I lost them one day. It was freezing cold, and I went searching, only to find the three of them huddled behind the catering van with a hip flask full of brandy. Well, not so full by the time I found them!

"What about me," I asked.

"You're too young," said Dad firmly.

"But I'm twenty!" I protested indignantly.

To no avail; I was still Daddy's little girl. However, the Yetis were much more accommodating and used to surround me to keep me warm! I think they were actually quite a sweet looking monster, rather cuddly. Not that I showed that on screen of course!

Another member of the guest cast on this one was Vic Pemberton's friend David Spenser as Thomni. David was a great giggler; I literally couldn't look at him without setting either myself or him off. Gerry got quite cross with us because we were incapable of doing a scene together. I had to deliver all my lines looking slightly away from his face to avoid cracking up.

The Abominable Snowmen saw Martin Baugh taking over costume design on the series, so the outfit I wear in the infamous shoot from the location filming was his creation. He asked me what I thought about wearing plus fours, boots, big socks and a little jacket and I said yes; at least I could move about, and it was practical for the running. It was also quite tomboyish, but I think that worked really well. It also spared me the indignity of running around in a miniskirt! Martin was a brilliant designer and I used to have a large input into what I wore. We'd decide between us what Victoria would wear, and if I didn't like something, I wouldn't wear it. I know quite a few of the *Who* girls after my time didn't have such an easy ride with their costumes, but I was very lucky because he was sympathetic to my ideas.

I also struck up a tremendous friendship with my wardrobe lady, a woman by the name of Lynda Keetch, who was the same age as me. She had a house in Ealing, so I would often stop over during filming on the show to save having to drive home. I recall the first time I stopped there, a little while into my time on the show. Her brother Anthony was all of five years old and a tremendous fan of the series. I parked up, walked up the pathway and rang the doorbell. Anthony answered, took one look at me, went white as a sheet, screamed and ran upstairs to lock himself in the loo. It took him three weeks to speak to me! Kathy and Wilf, her parents, were also living there, so we formed a strange sort of family unit.

The pair of us used to holiday together, and eventually we moved into a flat, still in Ealing. I don't know how we got along because we were like chalk and cheese, but it worked so well. Sadly, as is often the case, we grew apart. I was busy in the theatre and she moved to Devon to open a wool shop, but we continued to write to each other.

About two years ago I took a telephone call telling me that Lynda had died. It was an aneurysm. I was completely speechless. She was the same age as me, so full of life, and it had come right out of the blue. I went to the funeral, where her sister Judy read the eulogy. I was mentioned a lot in that reading, and it was all because we'd met on *Doctor Who*. Which led me to thinking what sort of impact the series has had on my life. There are many wonderful and happy memories, but equally there are some very sad ones which come into my mind when thinking of the programme, something stirred up whilst writing this book.

Continuing what was quite rightly to become known as the "Monster Era" was my next story, *The Ice Warriors*, which saw the introduction of the dreaded Martian invaders headed by the not-so-dreaded Bernard Bresslaw! I couldn't believe that dear Bernie, who was so well known from *The Army Game* and the *Carry On* movies, had been cast in *Who* and then promptly covered with a thick fibreglass helmet so you couldn't see his face. The poor fellows inside those costumes suffered with the heat, and the inability to be able to take loo breaks very easily. The heat inside the costumes also had the adverse effect of making the plastic eye covers steam up, meaning that they couldn't actually see where they were going most of the time. In one scene Bernie, as Varga, had to capture me and drag me back to his spaceship, through the ice tunnels.

Everything was cued up and ready to roll when he started to panic.

"I can't do this," he said in my ear. "I can't see where I'm going!"

So I came up with a solution. Instead of pulling me away, resisting furiously, I suggested I could walk in front with Bernie pushing me with his claw from behind. That way I could hold onto his claws and squeeze them for guidance, and mutter stage directions under my breath. We squared this with the director, Derek Martinus once again, and all seemed to be going well on the take.

"Action!" cued Derek.

And so we began winding along the ice tunnels: "left" squeezing the left claw, "right" squeezing the right claw, "right" squeezing the right again… Perfect. Until he misheard and went right instead of left. Six foot five, clad entirely in fibreglass, he lumbered straight through the polystyrene "snow" wall and brought the cave set crashing down around our ears! The poor prop boys were stood around with their heads in their hands, thinking how long it would take to restore it all. Bernard emerged from the wreckage totally oblivious to the dramas.

"Was that a good shot?" he asked.

Bernard was a great lover of the theatre. He did his *Carry On* work and the other more commercial parts, but always returned to what was his first love, the stage, doing some remarkable turns in Shakespeare. I was lucky enough to star with him in *Cinderella*, where he played an Ugly Sister. What a sight that was! The first time I saw him in his costume was for the dress rehearsal for the hunting scene in the woods. Joe Black, the great northern comedian, was playing the other Ugly Sister. In walked Bernie. Well, I mean he was a big enough fellow anyway, but now he was clad in knee length stiletto boots, fishnet stockings and suspender belt, the tiniest of miniskirts, asphyxiatingly tight corset, and a huge hat and wig. All that, and a whip!

"You're not going on like that are you?!" I asked, completely awestruck.

"It's great isn't it!" he replied gleefully.

It was quite a vision. And quite a horrifying one when he had to bend over during the scene.

"Bernie, you're going to have to stay up straight," I told him.

"Why?"

"Because we can see your tackle! It's a family show and you'll frighten the kids!"

Also in the guest cast on *The Ice Warriors* was the lovely Angus Lennie, a cheeky little chap who went on to find greater fame in *Crossroads* as Shughie McFee. He was another giggler, which caused no end of problems on set, I can tell you!

Peter Barkworth, who had the main part as Leader Clent, was a great mate of my dad's and had worked with him for many years on *The Power Game*. In fact he'd been in my scenes with me when I'd made a guest appearance in the episode *Late Via Rome*. I'd also worked with him on an episode of *Out of the Unknown*, where I played a scientist with copious amounts of technical jargon to spout. I actually contracted suspected appendicitis on that occasion, meaning I was out of rehearsal and only made it back on the day of recording. But I did it, straight off the top of my head, and he was very complimentary about it – and slightly dumbfounded that I'd managed to put in a performance at all, let alone one which he thought so good. That meant that this was the third time I'd got to work with him, although he suffered somewhat with a silly all-in-one white suit. Such were the sixties visions of the future!

❧

Doctor Who attempted to go a bit James Bond for the next story we made, and it counts as my least favourite adventure. *The Enemy of the World* was based around the notion of the Doctor having a doppelganger, the evil Salamander, which meant Pat got to play two parts instead of one, adding to the strain put on him no end. I don't think I can clearly say why it was my least favourite, but something about the whole thing just didn't click somehow. I remember going into the rehearsal rooms and Pat was the Doctor first, then he went into Salamander with the most extraordinary foreign accent. We were so used to him playing the Doctor, it took us all aback somewhat. Frazer looked at me and I looked at Frazer and we started laughing.

"You're not going to play it like that are you Pat?" we asked.

"Why, what's wrong with it?!" he intoned.

Of course, by the recording things had become even more pronounced. As Salamander, Pat had a Brylcreemed side parting and blackened thick eyebrows which met in the middle to make him look more like a sinister dictator. He got away with it, and people loved it, but to me the storyline just wasn't very good.

One benefit of the not-so-great story was that Victoria was imprisoned by Salamander, meaning that I got a week's holiday. This was something of a rarity as we shot one episode a week: rehearsal all week, then recording on a Saturday. With *Doctor Who* in those days we literally shot week after week because the regular characters were always needed. This had a particularly adverse effect on poor Pat, and I know he was already thinking of leaving the show by this point because the workload was so heavy for him. Remember, there were two companions to share the dialogue, but only one Doctor, so there was a tremendous amount of pressure on his shoulders for him to carry it along.

In keeping with the James Bond theme, *Enemy* had in its cast a very glamorous lady by the name of Mary Peach. Mary was a beautiful-looking lady with a wonderful figure. She played the leather-clad heroine, Astrid, and I can recall being distinctly jealous of her gutsy character, although I doubt very much whether Victoria would have suited a catsuit and kung-fu! It was slightly galling, though, because I was never really allowed to make Victoria as spunky as that. I was the pretty girl next door, there to be scared and scream at the Cybermen rather than kicking them. I tried whenever possible to make Victoria a bit of a tomboy, such as in the great scene in *Tomb* where I got to hold a gun and shoot the Cybermats. But such scenes didn't really come around often enough for my liking.

We were very lucky with our guest actors. There was a genuine family atmosphere as we worked through the week on rehearsals and then had our long recording day on the Saturday. Visiting actors would invariably have a ball, but there was an exception on *Enemy*: Colin Douglas. I was standing watching Colin rehearse a scene where he was seated behind a desk being very serious, and when he had finished he came over and we started to chat.

"So how are you finding it then?" I asked.

"I hate it. It's so boring," he replied dryly.

"Really?" I was surprised.

"It's the worst thing I've ever done, I'm certainly not coming back and don't want to be asked."

Well, that was that! He carried on and turned in a fine performance, but hated every minute of it. I was astonished to find that contrary to his word he did come back and made another story with Tom Baker a decade later. At the opposite end of the scale was a lovely Australian gentleman by the name of Bill Kerr, who made his name starring opposite Tony Hancock. Tony had rather unkindly had him forced out of the series when he became "too funny". That wasn't a problem for us; Bill fitted into our gang straight away and definitely enjoyed his six weeks on the series!

Another problem with the story lay with the director, a man who will be very familiar to fans of *Doctor Who*, Barry Letts. Barry went on to produce the series when Jon Pertwee took over, and very successfully so; but this was one of his first directing assignments, if not his first. He did not ingratiate himself at all well with the regulars. We rehearsed in a small church hall, and to the side was a room where we would play cards between scenes. Barry got fed up with this quite quickly because we were always late for our scenes, and tried putting his foot down. It didn't work. As much as you have to respect your director, and it is very important to do so, the director has to respect the actors too. With *Who* we were the regular team and we had our set ways, if you like, and as a visiting director he didn't like the set-up one bit and was quite a toe rag! Thankfully, and through the magic of fandom, I met Barry many years later at a *Who* convention and he was lovely: very warm, and it was a pleasure spending time with him and his wife, so perhaps he wasn't himself when he did *Enemy*.

Enemy's cliffhanger segued straight into the following story, yet another six-parter, called *The Web of Fear*. I remember recording that scene in the TARDIS where we're on the floor holding onto the console so we don't get sucked out into space. Of course it was all on the flat with a tilted camera, but it worked well, and by some miracle I managed to keep my modesty in my miniskirt, as Frazer did in his kilt!

Having found Barry a little lacklustre, it was brilliant to have Douglas Camfield on board for this one. Dougie was a lovely man and when we had rehearsal breaks we'd have a coffee and he'd play his guitar; he always had his guitar on set. Dougie was a very sociable director, but had a clear idea of what he wanted to get from you in your performance. Because he was so kind and so brilliant at his job we all went that extra mile to make sure he got it. He brought something out in you as an actor that made you believe you could do more than you would try normally. He was one of us, not strict, or dictatorial, and certainly never waved a baton from behind a music stand. He was just Dougie, and we all respected him.

For me the big news about *Web of Fear* was the return of my father playing Professor Travers. As the story was set quite some time after *Abominable Snowmen* it was necessary to age

Dad up with make-up, half-moon glasses, walking stick and a hat. He also gruffed his voice to make him more crotchety and gave a very good character performance. Pat, Frazer and myself couldn't stop giggling, perhaps even more so than we had at Pat's Salamander getup!

Of course, with the reunited gang of Pat, Frazer and my father, it wasn't long before I was on the receiving end of the mickey-taking once more. One particular scene had the terrible trio in search of Victoria, who had been kidnapped by the Yeti. They made their way along the London Underground tunnel: Pat in the lead, followed by Frazer, then Father. The trio stopped suddenly when they spied a dainty lace handkerchief on the lines.

"Victoria must have come this way," Pat said, leading them further on, ad-libbing all the way. Pat was a terrible one for ad-libbing. You never quite knew where he was going to go with it, and he'd often not give you your cue, so you'd literally have to wait for him to stop talking and just fire your line! Anyway, they kept moving along the tunnel, until Pat stopped suddenly.

"Aha! Victoria definitely came this way!" he declared, lifting a pair of frilly knickers off the line. "These are hers!"

Watching off camera I began, as usual, to go a slight shade of crimson.

"Och aye, they're hers all right," chipped in Frazer, taking them off him.

"HOW DO YOU KNOW?!" boomed Father.

We all creased with laughter, including Dougie. We could have all been in a lot of trouble for such a prank, but Dougie thought it was just the funniest thing. So it became a running gag on the production. I remember at one point Pat reaching into the Doctor's coat for a handkerchief and pulling out another pair of knickers and mopping his brow with them. The teasing was relentless!

For fans of the series, however, the big news was the introduction of a character called Lethbridge-Stewart. Colonel in this, but later and more infamously to become Brigadier.

Apparently the original actor cast was David Langton, who had played my father in *Alice*, but when this fell through the part went to Nicholas Courtney. I remember Nick walking into the rehearsal room. He was a young, handsome man, and I think he knew it; he liked his ladies! Another actor in this later to get some military promotion was John Levene, who went from Yeti to Sergeant! Ralph Watson was another very dishy member of the cast, and I recall having a crush on him. As a result I went to see him in a play in Hornchurch where I sat in the audience and admired how gorgeous he was. Ralph, bless him, caught wind of this burgeoning fascination and was forced at one point to tell me to calm down. I used to follow him round the studio like a puppy, such are the follies of youthful crushes!

As usual with *Doctor Who* locations, my final story, *Fury from the Deep*, was shot not in warm sunny climes, but on the British coast in winter. We filmed *Fury* down on Margate beach in the absolute freezing cold. My skirt was so short on this story! I remember seeing it when it was broadcast and there was a shot where the Doctor, Jamie and Victoria are going towards a door. It was framed from the rear and the two guys were in front of me, and I was very surreptitiously adjusting my skirt, trying to pull it lower because I was so self-conscious. I absolutely loathed it being so short! Frazer was very protective over me and what I wore, and would tell me if he thought something wasn't right. Not in a nasty way, more because he was looking out for me. Then Pat would tell him to stop interfering and leave me alone, and I'd be caught in the middle of a mini-argument, albeit a light hearted one.

The opening scene of the serial involved the three of us having to disembark from the TARDIS (which had landed on the surface of the sea) and sail to shore in a small dinghy with our lifejackets on; we then had to walk along the shore, ad-libbing away about the weather and the sights, before we stumbled upon some foam and investigated. Now, as it was absolutely perilously cold, and I was in the skimpiest of gear, I decided I would stand on the periphery of this foam, and told Pat and Frazer this, because I didn't want to get soaking wet as well as being cold. They agreed, and so we went for a take. By this point the public had got wind of the fact that we were filming there, as they often did, and were standing around watching intently. The camera was fixed into its set position, so once we started rolling there could be no chance of going back.

"You and Frazer go into the foam, and I'll stand and ask what you're doing," I reaffirmed as the director, Hugh David, called "Action!"

Pat and Frazer began playing around in the foam, splashing it around and dancing about like a couple of school kids. Then they stopped. And looked at each other. Then they slowly turned to look at me, and began to advance. I knew I was in trouble. I couldn't move and they were coming for me. They each took hold of me and dragged me into the middle of this sopping wet foam and proceeded to give me the birthday bumps, up and down, up and down, until I was totally plastered with the stuff. I stumbled out of the centre absolutely covered, like a foam monster, my costume wet through and coated with sand. Hugh was pleased though.

"Wonderful idea, love it," he said, as I made my way towards a dry towel.

I didn't swear in those days, but I did give Pat and Frazer a very hard stare.

"You beasts!" I told them.

Not that they showed any remorse. In fact the more I told them off, the harder they laughed and the harder everyone else did too.

"I hate you, don't you ever do that to me again!" I continued indignantly.

"What a great idea," laughed Hugh, walking over to us. "But there's a problem."

"What?"

"Someone behind the camera laughed."

"I beg your pardon?"

"A member of the public. Laughed during the take and you can hear it, so we're going to have to go again from the top."

So it was back to the coach for a rub down, clean up and then I had to go through it all over again!

We stayed at the local hotel; there's always a lovely atmosphere when everybody is encamped together, eating in the same restaurant in the evening. One person I remember very clearly from the shooting, not least from his antics in the bar, was a man by the name of Mike Smith. Or rather "Mad" Mike Smith as he was better known. Let's say he had his quirks. It was his job to do all of the helicopter work involved in the serial, and I was very nervous about going up in one for the first time. Actually that brings to mind another example of Frazer's ungentlemanly conduct! I confided in Frazer that I wasn't too keen on going up in a helicopter. It was one of those small bubble affairs, and I was quite convinced that it wasn't very safe with the open sides. Anyway, I took him to one side to explain the problem.

"Frazer, when we run to the helicopter, can you let me get in first please?" I asked. "Then I can sit between you and the pilot."

"Of course you can, little Debs," he replied, patting me protectively on the back. "No problem at all."

Well, to be honest I should have known. Hugh called action on the shot and we both broke into a run. Frazer, however, had suddenly discovered an Olympic calling and literally shot off into the distance; I had never seen him run that fast! The bugger wouldn't admit that he was scared of heights and so made sure that he was in the middle, with me on the outside. I remember trying not to look down at the great expanse below and clinging onto Frazer's arm for dear life. We had no seat belts whatsoever; I mean health and safety would have a blue fit nowadays. Mike piloted this thing at a sharp angle and then slowly brought us down on top of a cliff. My nerves were shattered.

"That was fun, wasn't it?!" announced Mike with a gleaming grin.

"No it wasn't," I pouted. "I want to get out."

But the boys had other ideas! Frazer clamped onto my arm and Mike took off once again, shooting up into the sky. We had a detour all around the coast for what seemed like forever, before being deposited safely back down on the beach.

Anyway, Mike took a bit of a shine to me and asked if I'd like to have a drink in the bar one evening. I accepted and we arranged to meet up around eight o'clock. He was already there waiting for me, so I asked for a wine and he ordered himself a neat brandy. Nothing unusual in that. What *was* unusual was that he downed the brandy in one large gulp and then proceeded to eat the glass. He didn't smash it into pieces, he just started to take bites out of it and then swallow them. It became glaringly obvious that he was a total nutter! He kept going for over half an hour doing this; I couldn't tell you how many brandies he necked, each time repeating the same process and eating the glass afterwards. I seem to remember he ended the evening swinging from a chandelier in the middle of the lounge at the hotel and literally bringing the roof down. Mike told me he wanted to fly me home to Alderton Hall in his helicopter and land in the back garden. I had to politely explain the logistics of why this wouldn't work, not least how I'd explain it to Father, and remind him that I was rather fond of driving my own car. For the record it was a little red Spitfire, which was my first car, and I totally adored it. LNO 400C was the registration; you always remember your first registration plate!

æ

Of course, *Fury* was to be my last story. I think I made my decision during filming on *Web of Fear* and told them that when my contract ran out I was off. Pleasantly, I already knew and had worked with my replacement, the equally diminutive

Wendy Padbury. Some years earlier we'd co-starred in a touring production of *The Roar of the Greasepaint – The Smell of the Crowd*. We were little urchins in the chorus! There were three of us who shared a room whilst doing that; myself, Padders and Sheila White. We were only about sixteen or something at the time. Frazer of course was delighted with my replacement, and was straight in! It eased some of the pain of leaving to know that I was handing over to a very talented and lovely lady, although I have a terrible confession to make here. *Doctor Who*, as I have said earlier, was very much seen as a children's show. Nothing wrong in that at all. On the last day of my filming Wendy came along to say hello and catch up, and I had something to ask her. She had just finished working on a film called *The Prime of Miss Jean Brodie*, which had been a huge success, so I wanted to know why on earth she wanted to do *Doctor Who*! It sounds terrible now, but in those days there was a prevalent attitude that film was much more worthy than television, and moreover drama more worthy than children's drama. Nowadays you get far more cross-over, certainly between film and television; but there was a certain "snobbery" if you like back then. Little did I know then quite how long *Doctor Who*'s popularity would endure!

Patrick was never terribly well when we were making the series. One day we had a break from rehearsals at the BBC and he was standing outside on the balcony. I looked at him and he didn't look right at all.

"Are you okay Pat?" I asked worriedly.

"No, I'm not," he rasped. "I'm getting terrible heart palpitations."

"You must go to the doctor," I told him.

He really did have a heavy workload. The doctor put him on pills, and he got better, but wasn't quite the same again. I think it frightened him quite a bit, understandably so, and he knew I was very concerned. When I left the show Pat wanted to leave with me; he couldn't bear the thought of me going. But he did stay on, and I know he regretted it. That's nothing against Padders, whom I adore, but he simply didn't want to continue to make that third year. I had to leave, as I have said, but we kept in touch, and saw each other from time to time, perhaps not as much as we should have.

It was many years later when I was playing in Swansea that I heard the news that he'd passed away. I was driving back to London listening to the evening news, and the headlines were being announced.

"...and one of TV's Doctor Who's has died," came the announcement.

I knew it was Pat, I just knew it. I pulled over to the side of the road to listen, and after the other stories had been read out it came to that piece: and yes it was true, Patrick Troughton had passed away in America. I was so sad. Tears began streaming down my face; I don't know how I managed to drive home, but I had to. But then all the good times came flooding back to me, all the happy times we'd shared. Pull yourself together Watling, I thought; he was a great actor who'd had a fabulous career and been a wonderful friend. Then I started to think through all our experiences together and I found myself smiling. Of course I was going to miss him; I still do. I have a picture of him on the wall in my kitchen, and I look at it even now, twenty-three years on, and smile and say hello to him. You never quite get over a loss, do you? He took me under his wing for my year on *Who* and kept me protected, and I shall be forever thankful for that. He was a very special man and will never be forgotten, by me or by the fans.

Chapter Four

I honestly thought that I had got out of *Doctor Who* in good enough time for it not to affect me by way of typecasting. I had gone in, done my year, and come straight out again, from April 1967 right through to March the following year. But I was wrong, very wrong. I was completely out of work for nine months. Not a scrap. This handicap was compounded by dear Auntie Beeb deciding to make the revolutionary move of repeating *The Evil of the Daleks* just after Wendy's first story. I gather that this is the first time they had ever repeated a story in its entirety; and as it was going out on a weekly basis, to all intents and purposes it still appeared that I was the current *Who* girl. So much for shaking off the image and moving on!

It was therefore time to pursue a different avenue, as actors often do in the grandly named "fallow" periods. Father had a tailoring business in Buckhurst Hill, run for him by a man called Eddie. Eddie sadly turned out to be a less-than-honest fellow, with hands in the till, so Dad decided to close it down. With my career on a sudden hold, I saw the opportunity to branch out, and offered to take over the business and run it as a boutique. A best friend of mine called Joan had moved out to South Africa after leaving school and run a clothes shop over there, and was now returning to England. So I asked her if she would like to help me run it using her experience, and she agreed. So The Pink Clock was born!

Unfortunately by the time we opened the boutique the sixties had stopped their swinging and the day of the miniskirt was nearing its end. Whereas it had been all the rage to have hip and happening little shops in the mid-sixties, we were just over the tip and on a terrible slide of unpopularity. I explained to Joan when we started out that my acting career would have to come first. If I got an audition, or a role in a production, then the business would have to take a back burner with me. She was fine with this, and confident that she could carry on in my absence and keep things ticking over (no pun intended). Sure enough, after a few months, a role did come along, a major one, meaning I had to take leave of the business to concentrate on acting once more.

It was for a BBC 1 soap opera called *The Newcomers*, which was a kind of sixties equivalent to *EastEnders*. Indeed the late Wendy Richard was amongst the first cast in it. I was lucky enough to be cast alongside my dad again, but joyously this time we were actually playing father and daughter. This was great because you got a sort of inbuilt chemistry, understandably so! This was helped further by the casting of Mary Kenton as my mother in the series, as Mary was actually one of Mummy's best friends in real life. I recall we three spoke standard English, but there were twins cast as my two brothers who spoke with very heavy cockney accents, which must have seemed quite bizarre to the viewing public! *The Newcomers* was shot up in Birmingham in a converted cinema, and was quite a quirky little set-up, although long gone now. Also in the cast was the lovely Jeremy Bulloch, whom I would work with again later on, but who is probably best known as Boba Fett in the massively successful *Star Wars* films.

There was one scene I remember recording in particular where Father was standing in the middle of the garage playing with a train set whilst we had a heart-to-heart. It was quite extraordinary, because he used to play with his train set back at the Hall, so there was a definite blurring between fiction and reality. Daddy maintained that he'd bought the model railway for Giles, but we all knew he was a big kid at heart; if he ever went missing we could invariably find him up in the loft playing trains!

Well, I'm sorry to say that we went into *The Newcomers*, did it, and closed the series. I gather the series was already on a downward spiral; sadly, we didn't revive its fortunes and it came to an end. Not long before I finished on the show, I remember going back down to check on the boutique. As I opened the door I was greeted by a shocking vision of blue. The place was filled floor to ceiling with pair upon pair of jeans, like a Levi's warehouse.

"What on earth are all these?!" I asked.

"I got an amazing deal," said Joan, merrily stacking the overstocked slacks.

"Really?"

"Oh yes," she said proudly. "I got discount because they're all last season's jeans!"

"But you can't do that! Nobody will buy last season's clothes from a boutique!"

Things were exasperated further by the appearance of her boyfriend on the scene, who moved into the flat above the shop. Conversely, as the takings went down at the boutique so the flat above it grew to be more lavishly decorated with new curtains and so forth. Coincidence it wasn't. We fell out over it, and I ended up closing the shop. I lost so much money on the venture, a heck of a lot I'd saved during my career to that point; but worse still I ended up souring what was once a very great friendship.

There were other factors involved in the closure of The Pink Clock. One terrible thing was that I really couldn't serve in there. I just couldn't cope with serving the public. I mean people will think that bizarre: as an actor you're expected to be very personable and outgoing, which I think I can be, but not when trying to sell clothes! There was one particular instance when a rather generously sized lady came in to make some purchases.

"I would like to buy a dress," announced the plump lady.

"Certainly, have you anything in mind?" I replied, doing my best salesperson's bit.

"Where are your size tens?" she continued grandly.

I looked at her cautiously and surveyed the lumps breaking for freedom on her dress. Her hair was immaculately coiffured, and her hands and neck dripping with overstated gold jewellery. Affluent she may well have been, but she was not even close to a size ten. If she were to try cramming into one of the delicately made items on the rail... well!

"Would you like to try one of these?" I said, steering her gently towards our larger items.

"I want to try on your size ten dresses," she continued resolutely.

"Look, are you sure you're a size ten?" I said politely.

"Of course I am," she said with an air of haughty disgust. "I want to try a size ten."

I had terrifying visions of having to prise a zip up her back and seeing it rip before me.

"I think you might be better off trying a size fourteen," I offered firmly.

"A fourteen?!" she bellowed.

"Yes, we have several nice –"

"A FOURTEEN?!" she repeated. "I have never been so insulted in all my life! I wish to see the manager."

"You're speaking to her."

"Well the owner then," she continued, eyeing me up and down with suspicion and contempt.

"That's me," I said, standing my ground.

The woman was fit to bursting.

"I suggest if you wish to try a size ten, then you try another boutique," I advised.

With that, she turned sharply on her heel and left with a slam of the door, never to return again. Maybe customer service wasn't my forte!

It wasn't all doom and gloom at the boutique. One very amusing incident came with the shop's sign. Trying to capture some of the swinging sixties vibe, the whole shop front was painted a very vibrant pink, with a large clock and the shop's name The Pink Clock emblazoned at about shoulder height. One morning I was coming along the street, reaching into my handbag for the keys to open up, when I noticed some vandals had been up to mischief overnight. Very specifically they had stolen the "L" from the sign, giving the impression of rather a different sort of shop, and one which had old ladies going faint for the rest of the day!

One important part of my time on *The Newcomers* was meeting an actor by the name of Tony Verner. We met on set, fell in love and started to date. We were together for three or four years. He used to come down to the Hall and visit, but Father never approved; maybe because he was still married – separated, but still married on paper. He had a daughter called Katie who was born during filming on *The Newcomers*, and the two of them used to visit regularly. We even discussed at one point adopting her, but that never happened, thankfully in retrospect. Katie now works in the business. I remember years later sitting in my dressing room at a theatre in Canterbury with the door open. It was at the end of a long corridor and there was this figure of a girl charging all the way along and into my room. She was very tall, blonde and slim.

"Debbie!" she cried.

I looked at her with shock. It had been nearly twenty years.

"Katie!" I said, overjoyed at the reunion.

Things didn't really work out with Tony. He went off touring with a play and I went off touring with another, and in those days it was much harder to keep things going at a distance. I mean now there's mobile phones and email, but back then the communication just wasn't there. I also found my heart wandering in its affections to somebody new, and started seeing them. Tony was, understandably, not very happy and tracked me down. I was with my new man, an actor called Terence Longden, at his flat in London. Tony banged on the door maniacally, Terry opened the door and for a moment it looked like the two of them were going to have a fight. It got very ugly and I couldn't believe how badly I had let things go.

I still see Tony from time to time. He was a mad keen golfer, which made me a golf widow. We would go down to Richmond Golf Club with all his mates, including Terry Frisby who wrote the famous play *There's A Girl In My Soup*, which I appeared in many times. They were strange days. Outrageously walking round the course in my hotpants, getting wolf whistles off the appreciative and steely stares off the more majorly types who didn't approve of women being there under any circumstance, let alone provocatively dressed. But it was the seventies – that's what we did!

Hotpants on the golf course brings me neatly on to 1973 where I got to play crazy golf in ski pants on film. *That'll Be the Day* was a major production starring David Essex and former Beatle Ringo Starr. I had the call from my agent to go up and audition for the part of David's girlfriend, so along I went to meet the producer David Puttnam and the director Claude Whatham. In those days you always had a screen test when you were up for a major part, so I duly gave my all and ran through the various required scenes and shots. Puttnam came up to me as I finished and put an apprehensive arm around me.

"Great screen test," he said.

My confidence lifted.

"Really?"

"Oh yes, but there's a small problem," he said pensively.

"And what's that?" I asked.

TOP LEFT My father, the matinée idol
TOP RIGHT My mother aged twenty-two
BOTTOM LEFT Nanny in trademark hat and coat
BOTTOM RIGHT Me aged eighteen months

TOP LEFT Picking flowers with big sister Dilys
TOP RIGHT Mummy with my brother Adam
BOTTOM LEFT Me aged four
BOTTOM RIGHT A school photo

A welter of Watlings

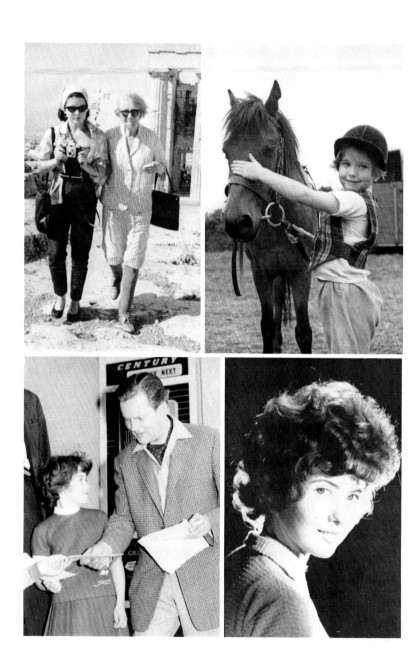

TOP LEFT On holiday with Nanny at the Acropolis
TOP RIGHT Misty and me
BOTTOM LEFT With Dad, signing autographs
BOTTOM RIGHT Teenage portrait

TOP LEFT An early promo picture for my agent Jimmy Vickers
TOP RIGHT A photo taken by my first boyfriend!
BOTTOM LEFT Mother and Father at Alderton Hall
BOTTOM RIGHT Theatre girl

Daddy's girl

TOP LEFT Marrying Nick
TOP RIGHT Marrying Steve
BOTTOM With my two husbands

TOP LEFT Me and Megs
TOP RIGHT Mother and Father
BOTTOM Golden Wedding celebration, 1997

"Well, we've auditioned you for the part of the girlfriend, and well…" He paused to form the words. "Well, you look a bit too knowing to play the innocent part," he continued.

Knowing?! I had never been called "knowing" before, but I continued to smile politely and nod as he spoke.

"But we'd really like you to do the film."

"So what part did you have in mind?"

"Ah, we have a cracking part for you!" he beamed. "She's called Sandra."

I read back through the script on the way home. Sandra, it transpired, was the saucy sort who becomes David's first lay in the film. I had never really done anything like that before. I may very well have looked "knowing" to Puttnam, but most other casting directors had placed me into the girl-next-door category.

One of the principal requirements for the role, aside from my "knowing" look, was to be able to jive properly. Upon confirmation from my agent that I was to play Sandra I was duly packed off to a dance centre in London to learn. This is where I first encountered David and Ringo, who had also been sent along. So I learnt to jive with the two boys, and believe me there are much worse ways to spend the day! Ringo was an unprepossessing fellow, with booming Liverpudlian tones. He had, for want of a better word, a simple air, not showy at all, which was amazing considering how successful he'd been with the Beatles and all the money and adoration he'd received. He was a legend! Yet here he was learning to jive and chatting away like an old acquaintance.

We filmed the whole thing on the Isle of Wight at a place called Shanklin. I was literally surrounded by a whole host of desperately famous musicians and actors, including Keith Moon and Billy Fury. David was a great family man, and had his wife and kids with him on location, but did not have them around whilst filming. It occurred to me that a lot of the musos were acting rather strangely. Being the naïve thing that I was, I couldn't really work out what it was that was making them act that way. Especially Keith Moon, who was completely nuts. Of course I came to realise that they were all, shall we say, using aids to enhance their performances? Albeit not medically recommended ones.

The cast always ate together at night, like a little family group. One night, after a particularly arduous day of filming, we settled down as usual for our evening meal. On this occasion, Keith sat at the head of the table and insisted that I sat on his left. David was opposite me, Ringo on my left, and a whole line of other people. It was a very posh hotel, so there was a certain standard of etiquette to be maintained. Not so for Keith. All the way along this great table at short intervals were these mighty flower arrangements. Large, multi-petaled, stem after expensive stem, clustered together in a delicate, beautiful manner. We were, as I said, all very tired, and very glad when our food eventually arrived. I had literally taken one mouthful when Keith sprang up out of his chair with his knife and proceeded to run the length of the table decapitating the flowers, showering everybody's plates with thousands of tiny petals. On top of that, he managed to knock over several vases, splashing water everywhere and smashing a couple. Our meals were utterly ruined! Keith laughed hysterically at this, thinking he was the great joker.

"You prat," I said, fixing him with an icy stare. "What on earth have you done that for? No one's amused."

"Oh c'mon Debs, it's funny!" he gurned.

"Fun? It's not bloody fun," I continued, shooting daggers at him. His smile evaporated. "Now you are going to order all of our meals again, and pay for them. And don't you ever, ever, do that again."

Keith sat back down in his chair like a severely scolded schoolboy.

"All right then. Sorry," he pouted.

Keith was a lovely guy really, but quite potty. He got slightly fixated with me during filming and would phone me up every night. On the hour. Literally! I'm not sure what substances were being taken, but they were certainly doing him no good. Nor were his phone calls doing me any good. He just didn't sleep.

"Debs, you up? Wanna come to my room?" he'd ask.

"No, I'm trying to sleep!"

"You don't need to sleep, come over to mine," he'd implore.

"No thank you, I have to do shooting in the morning," I'd insist.

"Oh go on, if you come over I'll give you one of my diamond rings, you'd like one, wouldn't you?"

"No thank you Keith, good night!"

In the end I got the girl on the switchboard to block my phone. It was the only way I was going to get any peace! I think he was a bit sad really. All the fame and fortune he'd found hadn't done him any good, and he didn't seem able to cope with what it had done to him and hid behind a mask of eccentricity.

Sandra was a great part to play. She was on holiday with her best friend, played by Patti Love, at a holiday camp full of dreadful old-fashioned chalets; just like the original Butlins. I remember my costume was very alluring: tight black trousers, a close-fitting black sweater to show off my assets, and some killer lashes. All topped off with a mighty seventies bouffant hairdo. Fabulous stuff! Of course Sandra was a total tart, and the scene I was dreading filming was the sex scene. I know a lot of *Who* fans have watched it, because I get asked about it a lot at conventions! In fact, I often get asked to say the infamous parting line, which I refuse, lest there be children in the audience. For those who haven't seen the film, after popping David's character's cherry, the mighty Sandra pulls a disgusted face and utters the immortal line:

"Do you always cum *so* quick?"

When we came to shoot the scene there was a fairly small chalet set, and in it were cramped the lighting people, the sound, the director... Quite daunting! People always ask what it's like to shoot sex scenes in films, and I can tell you it's the most non-sexual thing you can imagine. Claude Whatham was incredibly clinical in directing it, too.

"Can you put your right hand on her left knee and travel it up her thigh and under her skirt?"

It was like a dot-to-dot of sex.

"Now Debbie, you slide your left hand down his chest."

As you can imagine, not the most erotic of scenarios. However, when we came to do the actual take, Whatham gave the order to clear the set, leaving us with just director, one cameraman and one sound guy. David and I were feeling extremely nervous, just waiting to get it over and done and in the can. But Whatham wasn't quite ready to start recording.

"Do you two remember the film *Don't Look Now*?" he asked, leading the conversation.

"With Julie Christie and Donald Sutherland?"

"Yes, that's the one," he continued, nodding. "Well, they had a wonderful sex scene in that."

"Did they?" I asked, starting to get suspicious.

"Yeah," he stopped and looked at us both. "Do you know why it worked so well?"

David and I had no idea.

"No?"

"Because they did it for real."

I looked at him, then I looked at David, and a firm resolve came over.

"Well good for them. We're not going to!"

He actually expected us to have sex on set, for real! I certainly wasn't up for making porn, and neither was David! We were actors! Anyway, we lay back and got ready for the cameras to roll.

"You okay?" asked David.

"Not particularly," I answered. "You?"

"I'm terrified!" he conceded.

"Well, let's just get this over with!" I said.

Which of course we did. As soon as "cut" was called, Claude called out for brandy to be brought to the set.

"I don't need brandy," I protested. "I'm not in shock!"

That wasn't quite the end of the ordeal. A few weeks after we wrapped, Claude called me back in to do some extra dubbing. Nothing unusual in that; but it was for the sex scene, and I had to provide some additional heavy breathing. A very strange experience! Claude less-than-comfortingly told me just beforehand that David's wife had seen the scene and was not happy at all. In fact she was livid! As a result the scissors were taken to it, and it was pruned quite heavily.

The film has quite a big following; it's become something of a cult. One of the local policemen in my village, Steve, asked me if I had a copy he could borrow. I told him, sadly I didn't, so he rented it from the local video store instead. A week or so later his wife Jenny came up to me in the street.

"Steve borrowed that film," she started.

"Oh really?"

"And do you know what scene he keeps pausing it on?" she asked.

I knew straight away.

"The chalet scene?"

"Yes! When it gets to the shot where your nipple is on show he clicks to pause. He just stares at it for ages! 'That's Debbie's nipple,' he says."

"Well tell him to grow up!" I chided. The local copper, I ask you!

I think I had learnt very early on to overcome my embarrassment at having a sex scene on the silver screen. When the film was shown at my local cinema, Mother and Nicky, all of fifteen, went along to watch. I was away on tour, thankfully, and had no idea whatsoever that they'd been to see it. I came back to visit not long after when I had a weekend free.

"We saw *That'll Be the Day*," announced Mother, over breakfast.

Visions of romping with David Essex came flooding back.

"Did you?" I replied, keeping composed.

"You were very good, darling," she continued casually.

"You were," Nicky agreed.

"Well that's nice, thank you," I said and continued eating. "You liked it?"

"There's only one criticism I have to make," said Mother nonchalantly.

I paused crunching my toast.

"We didn't really like the heavy breathing."

There was no problem with heavy breathing in the next film I made. With Cliff Richard as the leading man? Certainly not! It just wouldn't be tennis! I was appearing in a play at the Theatre Royal Windsor when a call came through from my agent that I needed to audition. The theatre was run by John Counsell and his wife Mary, and I was playing opposite Mary as the maid in the piece.

"They want you to screen test with Cliff Richard for a film called *Take Me High*," my agent explained on the phone.

"Great," I said. Suddenly a thought struck me. "When do they want me to do that?"

My agent re-read the memo and broke the news that they wanted to do it on the opening night of my play. I was in turmoil. Obviously I wanted to do it, but I also categorically couldn't let John and Mary down. More than anything else, it's simply not professional. I went and spoke to Mary about it, and she was so understanding and told me I must go up for it.

"But I might miss the dress rehearsal!" I explained.

"Don't worry darling, we'll sort something out," she reassured me. "Somebody will read in for you."

So off I went to Elstree. I'd learnt the lines, the make-up girls had done their business and styled me for the role, then I had to wait for the scene to be set up. The whole time, the thought was running through my head that I wouldn't make it back in time and the play would be cancelled, and I'd be letting so many people down. I was really panicking. Eventually we completed the required shots, and Cliff looked down at me with a concerned look.

"Are you okay?" he asked.

"Well I'm in a play at Windsor, and tonight's our opening night, and I'm just really worried I won't make it back in time!" I blurted. "If I'm not there, there'll be no show!"

"Goodness me," said Cliff with great concern. "We've got to get you there straight away, you'd better go now. My driver will take you."

I thanked him profusely and was whisked away to the theatre. I rushed in and threw my costume on, literally just making my opening cue. The look of relief on Mary's face when I walked in was quite something.

"Thank goodness you made it!" she exclaimed.

During the run, the producer of *Take Me High*, Kenneth Harper, and the director David Askey came to see the show to see what I was like. Nothing unusual in that, but sadly the pair decided to sit on the front row. Actors can obviously see the audience as clearly as the audience can see them, which meant I could see them both looking at me for the whole performance. It was so off-putting, but I managed to make it through. It transpired that I was on their final shortlist, which had just two names left; Lesley Ann Down and Deborah Watling. Well, I thought Lesley was a stunning-looking lady and I wouldn't stand a chance. But they went for me, thankfully, maybe because I had more of that innocent look which would suit playing opposite Cliff.

So off I went on the journey up to sunny Birmingham, where the film was to be made. The plot, which was shaky at best, centred around the creation of a vegetarian burger called a "Brumburger", with a traditional romance tied in for good measure, and of course lots of songs. George Cole was cast in it, so it was great to have a familiar face on board; I had worked with him when I was about twelve when we'd done *A Life Of Bliss*. Anthony Andrews was also in it, and he was just starting to make his name. We of course went on to star together afterwards in *Danger UXB*. I can remember the explosion of publicity at the time, far more than with *That'll Be the Day,* mainly because I was playing one of the leads. Cliff was, and still is, very big news, so there was a great press interest which meant that there were plenty of photocalls, including a major one on a canal in Birmingham. Birmingham is famous for its canals, apparently.

The waterways were featured quite heavily in *Take Me High*. One scene called for my character to guide the barge as Cliff gamely went about his business of singing and being merry, with the occasional cut back to me looking innocent and loving. The big problem here was that I clearly couldn't steer a barge. I mean, why would I?! There was no time to give me any proper lessons, so I was duly given some simple instructions in preparation, but was far from confident about it all. When you steer it goes in the opposite direction to how you work the mechanism; if you pull left it goes right, and vice versa. There is also a slight delay before this kicks in, which makes it all the more difficult to ascertain whether or not you've pulled the lever in the right direction. The shot was actually meant to be quite a simple one. Cliff was to untether the boat, I'd pull away, chug downstream a little bit, under a bridge, then moor the other side. Easy! Well, no, not really. It was a beautiful sunny day when we came to record it, and everyone was packed on board the narrowboat; director, lighting, sound, and our continuity girl Gladys.

"Action!" yelled the director.

Cliff untied the ropes, leapt on board and I started to chug off down the water. I negotiated the bridge, and pulled in on the other side. Unfortunately I was a good six feet away from the bank. Ever the professional, and keen to complete the shot, Cliff went to jump on land.

"Stop!" I cried and pulled him back. "You'll never make it. Don't worry, I'll do it again."

So everything was reset and we went for a second take. It was all running so smoothly as I approached the bridge… then I misjudged it totally. The front of the boat went into the wall and CRASH! The crew toppled over, and there was an almighty sploosh as Gladys went backwards into the water.

"Help me, help me!" she cried, splashing her arms wildly in the water.

"I said I needed lessons!!!" I protested.

Poor Gladys, she had to be fished out and dried off, and I don't think she ever forgave me.

One of the side effects of the intense promotion surrounding the film was that the press office wanted Cliff and I always to appear together. When filming finished everyone would go out for food, but I would always have to be sectioned off with Cliff. They wanted to promote the idea of us being a couple off screen as well as on. The press would take photos of us hand in hand, and there would be the insinuation that we had fallen deeply in love, which was just ridiculous. Every evening we'd be sitting upstairs in a private room chatting away, all the time able to hear everyone else having a real party downstairs. Now Cliff is a lovely guy, but this went on far too long for my liking.

"Cliff," I said, breaking our conversation off one night.

"Yes Debs," he replied attentively.

"They're having rather a good time downstairs, aren't they?"

"Sounds like it," he shrugged.

"Well," I announced, placing down my cutlery. "I think it's about time we went down and joined in the fun."

Cliff looked a bit hurt.

"Nothing to do with you, you're a lovely man," I smiled.

"But what about the press office? They want us always to be seen together," said Cliff, concerned.

"Stuff it." Ever the rebel, I rose, stretched out my hand and led him downstairs.

From then on, that was it with the isolation. We were with everyone else, and had a much better time, rather than being publicity prisoners! I found the whole thing rather bizarre to be perfectly honest. He was a warm, gentle man, but there was just no way I was going to fall in love with him. There were plenty of ladies then who were, and many who still are, but it just wasn't going to be for us.

Cliff's admirers were a constant presence during the whole shoot. One particular instance sticks very firmly in my mind. We'd finished shooting for the day, and we had a couple of days free to go home. Cliff was going back to his country home, and I was off to visit Mum and Dad, so we decided to catch the train together. Off we went to Birmingham New Street, but very soon a crowd started to gather behind. Cliff had such a distinctive look, he couldn't just melt into the background. Masses of over-zealous girls were following us, shouting and screaming... like a hunting pack. It was so threatening.

"The train's in the platform," whispered Cliff. "When I say 'run', run, right?"

Well, I certainly didn't need telling twice.

"Okay," I nodded.

"Because these are going to get out of hand soon," he said.

Sure enough the pack started to get closer, and their cries louder and more aggressive.

"RUN!" he cried.

And we bolted. Straight down the concourse, leaping into a coach as it pulled out of the station, slamming the door firmly behind us with a reassuring lock. The girls had finally caught us up and started banging savagely on the windows, yelling and squealing. After a few moments we were clear of the station, and the pair of us just sat trying to catch our breath and calm down. It was a frightening and horrible experience, and I can't comprehend how he managed to cope with that on a regular basis. After a while I broke the silence.

"Well, I don't think I'll be travelling with you again!"

❦

The prop guys and the crew had been very courteous with me during filming. Perhaps the innocent girl I was playing was making them think I was made from fine china. These usually rowdy lads were doing their best to make me at home and treating me like a real young lady, offering me cups of tea and bacon butties.

"Hello Debbie, how are you?" they would ask. "Looking forward to a day's filming?"

They just couldn't do enough for me. Things were to change, however. During filming on *Take Me High*, the fruits of my last silver-screen encounter came to bear. *That'll Be the Day* was unleashed on cinemas nationwide, including, obviously, Birmingham. So which film did the crew go and see when they had a night off? I was completely oblivious, but the moment I walked onto the set next day I knew something had changed.

"All right darling?" called one bloke with a lewd wink.

I was most put out. I'd been sweet Debbie the day before; what had changed?!

"Pardon?" I replied aghast.

"All right sweetheart?" he smirked, nudging his mate. "Saw that film of yours last night. You know, that one with David Essex in."

In an instant it all made sense. Sweet little Debbie had now been very firmly tarred with the "knowing" Sandra.

"I hope you enjoyed it," I smiled.

"Oh yeah, we enjoyed it all right!" he grinned.

From then on they ribbed me mercilessly, but I enjoyed the banter.

Being a Cliff Richard film, *Take Me High* was laden with lots of songs. Indeed there was a full soundtrack album, which I only recently donated to the charity shop. Before filming began I went along to the Abbey Road Studios, which had of course been made famous by the Beatles a few years before, to show the producers what kind of a singing voice I had. It wasn't entirely uncommon for actors to be dubbed by someone else when it came to the musical parts, but they liked my voice and decided to record some tracks. Cliff and I stood side by side, singing away with our headphones on. Then we went in to hear the playback.

"Is that me?" I asked in surprise.

"Yes, you can sing!" laughed the producer.

"Good Lord!" I exclaimed.

Dilys had been signed up to a record company when she was younger, but I'd never really had any aspirations in that regard. The producers now wanted me to record a selection of songs for the film's soundtrack, some with Cliff, some solo. It didn't transpire that way, however. I got one song, a duet, and that was it. I certainly wasn't a threat to anybody, but words were spoken and my musical input reduced dramatically from what I'd been promised. I never got to the bottom of it, but it did gall me slightly, because I knew I could do it.

The one track which did get selected for use in the film was called *The Brumburger Duet*. Well, please. It was never going to top the hit parade, but it was fun to do with Cliff all the same. We shot the accompanying scene inside a studio-set version of the narrowboat as we prepared the aforementioned vegetarian treat in the kitchen. Obviously we had to lip-synch to the pre-recorded track, and Cliff told me that the best way to mime was to sing it for real because it looked more genuine. We did it in a couple of takes, and the scene culminated with our first kiss together. No tongues! We had another kissing scene later on in the movie, where I was on a swing with a rippling sun-glistened pond behind. Cliff was pushing me on the swing and we'd keep meeting and kissing, meeting and kissing and so on. In fact Cliff kept giving me a kiss every time the director called cut. I think I quite liked that, I know Cliff did!

We had our grand premiere back up in Birmingham a few days before Christmas 1973. The film had been financed by Billy Graham, the evangelist. Cliff of course was very heavily into religion and tried to talk to me about it one day. He soon saw I was a lost cause and didn't broach the subject again.

Take Me High was pretty much the worst film on general release in 1974. It absolutely bombed. Even the theme single failed to make an impact on the charts. This was no surprise to anyone. We all knew; after two days of shooting there was a general consensus that the final product was not going to be a smash. We had a great time making it, and the actors were all good – I mean the cast list included Anthony Andrews and Hugh Griffith for goodness' sake – but there was something lacking overall. Hugh Griffith, incidentally, was a filthy old so-and-so, and kept trying to touch me up in front of his wife.

"Take your hands off her," she'd shout. "She's not interested in you, you dirty old man!"

She would apologise, and I'd tell her it was okay and not to worry. There are so many characters you meet in the business, you kind of get used to such eccentric behaviour.

Chapter Five

I was working for Duncan Wheldon and Paul Elliot in a play called *Not in Front of the Parents* when the call came through from my agent that Duncan wanted me to go down to the Victoria Palace to audition for the part of Dorothy in *The Wizard of Oz*.

I wasn't overly enthusiastic at the idea. However, I duly went along as requested. Ordinarily when you audition there's a few of you sat waiting, and you go in, do your bit, then off. When I arrived at the theatre there were about three hundred girls all waiting to be auditioned for the part. There were so many there that not all of them were even going to be allowed to audition that day. Duncan wanted me back up for the evening performance of *Parents*, so I got thrust on and did some singing and dancing, showed off my American accent, then I had to read... It was quite heavy going, especially with all the other hopefuls watching you. Auditioning is nerve-wracking at the best of times; even worse when you can see the competition and they can see you.

So off I went back onto my tour, then I got another call asking me to go back the weekend after. This went on and on, and on and on, until finally there were just four of us left. Dad had arranged to pick me up after the final audition, and I remember being on stage and spotting him come into the auditorium. He spoke for a bit with Paul Elliot, then made his way down and sat in the third row. I was singing *Over the Rainbow*, and I looked down at him and he made a gentle thumbs-up gesture. I knew I had got the part.

There was a blaze of publicity for it; "the new Dorothy is Deborah Watling!" and "Debbie Watling is the new Judy Garland!" and so on. All totally overblown. They hyped it up so much, and I really began to feel the pressure. We only had two weeks of rehearsals before we opened, so I should have known something was up. Duncan and Paul confessed that they'd wanted me the whole time and had just done the auditions for the publicity. I was not pleased when I found out. The original director was awful and couldn't direct a thing. Desmond Walter Ellis, who was a big name in those days, was playing the Lion and he took over from the director. Thank goodness for Desmond! But he had so much to do, and so little time.

The first night came and expectations were very high. I made my big entrance and got a rousing ovation, which helped to settle my nerves somewhat. I launched into *Somewhere Over the Rainbow*, and it all went really well. The cast had all been kitted out with radio mics for the show, and one night I recall singing *Rainbow* and realising straight away that something had gone wrong. The radio mic had broken. Undeterred, I marched straight downstage to where there was a free-standing microphone and belted it out from down there. It was a close run thing.

"Why didn't it work?" I asked the sound guy.

"Well, er, it stopped," he replied helpfully.

From then on I totally refused to use the radio mics, and insisted on performing the song using a real mic at the stage edge. It was a horrible experience. And one which I think started to trigger quite a bad reaction. I felt my nerve starting to go. This had never happened to me before, and it left me quite shaken. I began to dread walking through the stage door and would have terrible panic attacks before I went on. My understudy was always waiting in case I finally couldn't take it and had to step down, but she was never required. In truth I was probably not helping matters by stopping with my parents in Laughton; rising early to travel down, and then getting back late at night. I was running myself into the ground through stress and lack of sleep. I managed to pull it back, thankfully, and enjoyed the last few weeks on what had been quite a fraught and tiring run.

Less troublesome was my turn in *Doctor in Charge*, which was a great ITV comedy series starring Richard O'Sullivan, George Layton and Robin Nedwell. I won the role of the physiotherapist Emma Livingstone in two episodes. Emma was a very professional, prim young lady and I got to climb all over William Franklyn, giving a massage. I quite enjoyed rubbing my hands over his body! Robin's character took a shine to her, and in the last scene of the first episode, he takes her along to the doctors' ball. Unfortunately it turns out to be a none-too-salubrious affair and he tries to get Emma away as quickly as possible. Emma, however, is not the innocent everyone thought, and proceeds to dance… then jump on a table and perform a striptease! With my back to the studio audience, this meant that I had to take my top off in front of my fellow actors. The show was recorded before a live audience at the old LWT studios on the North Circular Road, so in their quest to preserve my modesty in front of the viewing public, wardrobe provided flesh-coloured cones to cover my boobs. They looked most peculiar, and I couldn't help thinking it would have been better to show off my nipples!

Not long after *Doctor in Charge*, Father and myself were invited to make a guest appearance on *The Generation Game*. It was hosted at the time by Bruce Forsyth, with his wife Anthea, and we were called upon to assist with one of the games. We performed different lines with a variety of accents. I recall being asked to recite Lady Bracknell's infamous "A handbag?" line from Oscar Wilde's *The Importance of Being*

Earnest, amongst others. *Generation Game* wasn't recorded at Television Centre at this time – we were at the studios in Shepherd's Bush – and although it was a fleeting appearance, it was an enjoyable one and Bruce was very welcoming to us.

Having enjoyed *Doctor in Charge*, I was pleased to be asked to appear in another ITV comedy series, this time *Rising Damp* with the legendary Leonard Rossiter. I had recently adopted a new peroxide look, so when I walked into the rehearsal room I gave the director quite a shock.

"I was expecting a dark Watling, not a blonde one," he said, surveying the new hairdo.

One never quite gets over the nerves of the first day on a job. It's rather like going back to school, with the butterflies in the tummy. I was introduced to the regular cast, including the striking Frances de la Tour, and of course Leonard Rossiter. Frances and I were like chalk and cheese, but got along together tremendously well. Leonard was a very shy and quiet man, until he started to rehearse. Then the Rigsby character came out, and he *became* Rigsby. Even during tea breaks he stayed in character. *Hello Young Lovers* was the title of my episode, and Adam Lewis played my fiancé in it. The scenario was that the pair of us book a room for the night, and it's presumed that we have just got married. I let it slip to Miss Jones that we're not married; she tells Rigsby, and he becomes determined to prevent us from having a night of passion out of wedlock.

Leonard was a nice man, but became rather besotted by me. I always used to drive myself to the studio and back from my bachelor pad in Wandsworth. One day I drove home, parked up, and went inside. Ten minutes later I looked out of my window and Leonard's car was parked across the road. He'd followed me back, and there he was just sitting in the driver's seat, looking up at my flat. What could I do? He was a really big star and I didn't want to offend him. But the problem persisted. Worse than that, it actually began to increase. So much so that I decided the best thing to do would be to speak to him at work the next day.

"Leonard, I need to have a word with you," I began, calmly. "Because I know you've been parking outside my flat… watching me. I want to know what you're doing?"

He remained still.

"I just wanted to check that you got back home safely," he replied.

I wasn't convinced.

"But you just sit there and watch," I said. "Come clean. What are you up to?"

Then came the great revelation that he was totally fixated with me. He said he couldn't get me out of his head. I didn't know how to handle this. He had a lovely wife, Mary, and a family, so it just wouldn't do. It had to stop. Unfortunately he managed to get hold of my telephone number and started to call me at home persistently, saying that his wife didn't understand him and such things. He did manage to pull himself together, but I can remember walking out onto the studio floor to record the episode, and he stood back, taking in a deep breath.

"You're beautiful," he exclaimed.

The episode was recorded for Yorkshire Television at a studio in Leeds. After recording we all went into the bar there, and I remember a rather pretty tall young man coming up to introduce himself. He was Mike Reid, the DJ and television presenter, and was recording a children's show in the next studio. He had flown over from Luxembourg where he DJed and we got on really well. So much so that he invited me to go back to Luxembourg with him.

"Come over to Luxembourg," he said on the phone.

"No, no, I really don't want to," I said.

"Please, come and visit me over here," he continued.

"No, no, I honestly can't."

"Look I don't normally ask, but I really want you to visit," he implored.

"No, I'm not coming!"

My decision was final. So he flew back to England, where we met up. Then he came back to Alderton Hall to meet my parents and the family, then I finally caved in and flew out to Luxembourg with him. We were together for quite some time, and it was a very happy relationship, but unfortunately the distance ended up getting the better of us, and we split. I still see him occasionally, as he lives quite close to me, and runs his own radio station.

Bequest to the Nation was a play about Nelson and his affair with Lady Hamilton, staged at the Theatre Royal Haymarket, in which I played the part of Betsy. It was written by Terence Rattigan, and his boyfriend Peter Glenville directed it. They proved to be quite a duo. We had rehearsed all week at the theatre when one morning we were gathered round in a large circle on the stage to take direction from Glenville. He arrived and sat down solemnly.

"You," he said, pointing at a boy in the cast.

"Me?" replied the youngster nervously.

"Yes you," he continued deliberately. "I want you out. You don't know the play. Out!"

This was totally out of the blue, and I didn't know where to look. Directors never behaved like this.

"Out?" asked the lad.

"Yes. You're sacked," he concluded. "Put your script under your chair and go."

The poor thing, Richard was his name, complied. He slowly stood up, left his script on the floor, and walked out.

"Sorry," he said meekly as he left.

This threw us all off balance somewhat. Not quite as off balance as when a replacement walked through the door a mere ten minutes later. Glenville had, it transpired, already cast somebody new before sacking Richard. It was utterly dreadful.

Anyway, rehearsals continued, but a few days before the first night some changes were made to the script and my part was cut down somewhat. I wasn't happy, as one wouldn't be if one's part is reduced, but I got over it. Further changes were afoot, as Glenville so kindly informed me on the day of our opening night.

"You know the scene between you and the young master? The seduction scene?" he asked during a break in rehearsal.

"Yes," I answered, fearing another cut.

"Well Terence has written another one, we're going to drop it in," continued Glenville.

"Oh all right, when are we going to put that in then?" I asked.

"Tonight." I looked at Michael, who was now playing the young master, in horror.

Talk about in at the deep end. So we went next door to the coffee bar, we learnt it, and performed it for the very first time that night, *opening* night.

Things were about to get a whole lot worse than the demands of Glenville, as I discovered when Mother called me one day at the theatre.

"Darling, have you offended anyone?" she asked tenatatively.

"No," I said pausing to consider. "Not that I know of anyway!"

"Well, I've just had a phone call."

"From whom?"

"They wouldn't leave their name," she continued. "But he said tonight when you're on stage he's going to be in the audience and…" Her voice faltered.

"And what Mother?"

"He says he's going to shoot you," she said, trying to remain as calm as possible.

I froze for a moment. Whatever I was expecting, it wasn't that.

Of course the guy was a total nutter, but the police had to be informed as a precaution. Nobody knew whether this man was of sick enough mind to actually carry out his threat, so there were searches backstage, in the auditorium and a police presence front of house. Not the most comfortable of environments in which to perform. The constant searching and visions of men in uniform about the place kept reminding me that it was me that was in trouble, it was me who was on the receiving end of this nasty threat. As the hours ticked on and that evening's performance began to draw closer I honestly began to question whether I could physically manage to go out on stage, all the time knowing that at any given moment some unbalanced stranger could just stand up in the darkened crowd and shoot me. One pot shot and I would have been gone.

I plucked up the courage and decided to go ahead with the performance. Mother and Father were deeply concerned; in fact poor Mother was quite hysterical. Father reasoned that he'd had several nasty instances in the same vein throughout his career which had come to nothing, so I should try not to worry myself. Besides, I wasn't going to let down either the rest of the cast nor the audience who had paid to watch, just because some unhinged fellow had threatened me. The nerves jangled all night. I kept wondering if or when, but nothing happened. Nothing at all. The man made no further malicious calls to myself or my family, and I was left in peace after a week or so of police supervision. It was a tiring experience having police at the stage door, and an escort to the tube or my car each day, but it was reassuring and I was grateful to them.

One slight aside which caused me some consternation during the run was my discovery that the actors were not paid as much as the stage management. I was appearing on stage for seventeen pounds a week, which it transpired was a lot less than what the technicals were on. To put that in some kind of context: when I was appearing in *Doctor Who*, I got the princely sum of forty-nine pounds a week for my services! An absolute fortune in comparison.

∂

I was employed a lot for stage work by Duncan Wheldon of Triumph Productions. One of these was a tour of *Not in Front of the Parents* in which I played opposite Jack Halbert. It was a light, fluffy affair, no real depth, but that was the way it was with a lot of plays in those days. Duncan and his partner Paul Elliot had me on their list of girls that "can do"!

One of the great delights that stage held over the screen was the opportunity to work with Father directing me. He directed me in a number of productions, including *Lloyd George Knew My Father* at the Lloyd Park Pavilion in Walthamstow where he directed a couple of summer seasons. I appeared as Sally, and it was written, I recall, by William Douglas Home. Dad also directed me in *Two and Two Make Sex*, where I was paired up with Terence Longden. Terry, as I have already mentioned, was my partner for a while and Daddy never really approved of the set-up. Not least because Terry was older than he was! I remember breaking the news to Father that Terry and I were an item.

"Terence Longden? Oh yes, I know him," he commented politely. "Never worked with him, but I know him, yes."

There was an uncomfortable pause.

"You really should bring him down to the Hall to visit; I'd like to meet him properly."

He was taking it remarkably well. Too well.

"And when he does come down, what do I call him? Granddad?"

Perhaps not.

Professionally I did not find it strange to work with Father; he was a very good and very kind director. There was never any question of conflict of interests, which one might expect when working with one's family. Whenever Father directed me, the company all got along fine, with one notable exception when I was in a production and the young man playing my boyfriend took against Father. He became strangely jealous and decided that I was getting all the attention and focus, when it should be on him. He began to rant and say that Father had no right directing the piece, which made the whole thing rather uncomfortable for me. We were mates and shared digs together, so it seemed completely bizarre that he should turn like this.

As a director, Dad knew what he wanted, albeit in a slightly muddled kind of way. He was a great believer, as indeed I am now when I direct, in guiding actors rather than giving them straight direction. It is far better to have an idea suggested, or to be steered gently along a particular path, than to be told "say this like this" or "do this move like this"; you have to trust the actor to be able to do their job as much as they have to trust that you'll make sure it looks the best it possibly can. Strict direction absolutely crushes creativity. I've appeared in many Ray Cooney plays, but have never been directed by him. The amount of actors who have shared horror stories of his precision direction is innumerable. He will literally count beats for you during scenes and tell you where the laugh is; pick up the phone, two, three, four, say the line, laugh, three, four… He even gives notes during the interval! I just cannot work under those kinds of conditions. In fact my dear friend Frazer Hines walked out of one of his productions because he just couldn't cope with it. Frazer never lets anybody down, but it was too much to bear. There really is a lot to be said for a good director!

I used to do a lot of comedies on stage, and it was a great thrill to be able to do *There's a Girl in My Soup* by Terence Frisby at the Theatre Royal because Terence was a golfing partner of my boyfriend Tony Verner. Tony and I actually lived in the flat above his house, so we were very well acquainted. Therefore it was an incredibly easy question when I was asked to take on the lead role, given that I was living in the same house as the author!

"I've been to see them and I'm going to be playing the lead in your play," I told him after I'd met the producers.

"Ha," he smiled. "This is going to be very interesting…"

I began to feel a little worried then!

Cast as the male lead was an actor called Frederick Jaeger. Freddie was, in the main, a very amenable kind of man. But he did have a rather nasty streak running down the middle, as I was to discover very early on. We had completed three weeks at Windsor and were then asked to transfer to Coventry. We agreed, and it was there, quite out of the blue, one matinee as I waited in the wings to go on, that he approached me.

"Without me," he said, "you'd be nothing on that stage."

"Pardon?" I answered, somewhat taken aback.

"It's my timing."

"What on earth do you mean, *your* timing?" I replied.

"My timing out there makes it; I get you your laughs."

"No you don't," I said, still somewhat puzzled as to where this had all come from.

"We'll see," he said, fixing me with a raised eyebrow.

For that performance he was utterly outrageous and totally unprofessional. He changed his timing completely, he changed his moves, and when that hadn't caused quite enough problems he began changing lines. Of course it threw everyone on stage and made the whole thing look an entire shambles. I was most angry because the audience who had paid to see a professional production had no idea what was going on, and there was no way of letting them know it was simply Freddie being vindictive. I felt my blood boiling as we continued, and I nearly broke when he shifted one move to the opposite end of the stage. I took his arm and dragged him to his mark.

"Bloody stay there," I hissed.

The cast off stage had been following everything over the tannoy in the dressing rooms and were now gathered like a second crowd in the wings, waiting to see what would happen. As the curtain duly fell on the performance, I was shaking with rage.

"Don't you ever, *ever* do that again," I said with biting scorn.

"It was a lesson, wasn't it?" he replied, smugly.

"Not a terribly good one. Not from you." And with that I turned my back on him and left the stage.

It was no great thrill that I was going to be stuck with him doing the play for the next three weeks. However, we cleared the air and managed to continue without any further problems. Perhaps he was just bored, who knows. But needless to say, no matter what jokes you wish to play on each other on stage, it should never be at the expense of how the production looks to the public.

It was actually during the run at Windsor that Father asked me to be in his production of *There's a Girl in My Soup* at the Lloyd Park Pavilion. Terence Frisby was going to be directing and starring as the lead in his own play. As I have already said, starring in a play whilst lodging with the author is one thing, but starring in two productions, with different moves, directors, actors, at the same time… well it was utter madness! But I said yes, which meant I was rehearsing at Lloyd Park during the day and performing at Windsor at night, and was totally exhausted.

On the first night with Terence, he was visibly nervous. He was shaking, sweating, and had a look of pure terror in his eyes. I remember thinking how I was going to have to kiss him at one point during the play, and as I got close he was just soaking with sweat. That took some acting, I can tell you. Terence had been a difficult director with an overly dictatorial way of ordering actors into position and telling them how to say their lines, but I still felt sorry seeing him looking so bad, and turning in such an awful performance. This sympathy was to disappear rapidly as we gathered backstage after the first night.

"Right," he announced with an icy authority. "I want you all to go home tonight and learn the script." He turned back and stared at me. "And that means you as well."

I won't stand for that kind of nonsense from anyone.

"After the performance you just gave?" I said with a laugh.

His face dropped and turned an attractive shade of crimson.

Thankfully the run was only for a week, but I was still living above the man, which made it quite uncomfortable socially. Tony was away on tour, and one night I lay in bed and could hear someone very softly walking up the stairs. I began to doze off, but became aware of somebody getting into the bed next to me. I rolled over and opened my eyes. It was Terence.

"GO AWAY NOW!" I bellowed at him.

You might think I would have been more jumpy at the notion of a night-time intruder. But this wasn't in fact the first time it had happened at the loft conversion. Terence would often hold quite boisterous parties downstairs, and on one occasion I was awoken by the light up the stairwell shining through my door. I spotted a shadow on the wall and followed it down to where a figure was kneeling praying by my bedside.

"What on earth are you doing?" I asked.

He looked up at me. It was an actor by the name of John Standing.

"I'm praying," he rasped.

"What?!" I said confused. "Just go away!"

"I'm praying for you," he uttered. "Because you're beautiful!"

Something one has to deal with an awful lot in the business, other than actors and their foibles, is agents. My first was the same as my father's, Jimmy Vickers, and that worked out well. In fact my Auntie Connie worked at the same agency, keeping it in the family! But as an actor one is constantly looking to reinvent and try new things, so it's necessary, I think, to change management and see what sort of perspective or spin they want to give on your career. It takes a while after signing up with a new agent to establish a rapport; you have a few meetings to discuss ambitions and what direction you wish to take, but then it's up to them to find you the right openings for where you need to go.

A good agent will ring you during quiet spells to explain why there's nothing coming up. A bad agent will ignore you totally. Well, I've had a mixed bag of them, I can tell you. My second representative was part of a much bigger organisation and his name was Tim Wilson. Unfortunately, I did not realise he was an alcoholic, and therefore not capable of looking after himself, let alone my career. Work simply wasn't coming in and I would keep phoning and pestering, with absolutely no joy.

"I've put you up for a musical," he'd offer desperately.

"A musical? I don't particularly like musicals!" I would protest.

"Well, I've put your name forward now so you'll have to go for it anyway."

This went on for months and months, and then I was told he'd been hospitalised. It was then that I found out about his drink problem; it had got so severe he'd literally drunk himself sick. Thankfully he came out of hospital not too long after and went into the BBC working as a booking agent. Having dried out completely, he set up his own agency, and gave me a call inviting me to see him. Reluctantly I went over, we had some tea and he looked at me.

"Debs, I'm better now… I'd like you to come back to me," he asked.

"I don't think so," I replied, remaining as polite as possible. "It didn't really work out last time."

He took this statement with remarkable calm, and shifted in his seat slightly.

"I've got a confession to make," he said, glancing at me nervously.

"Oh yes, and what's that?" I braced myself.

"I ruined your career." He was ashen-faced.

"Yes, I think you did," I answered, calmly. "So if you think I'm coming back to you, you've got another think coming!"

With that I stood up and left. News reached me a year later that he'd passed away. It was such a tragic story.

Marjorie Armstrong was my next agent and also looked after a number of different people, including Henry McGee, which is how I met him. Mark Furness used to have some offices near the Garrick Club in Covent Garden and he cast the two of us in a play together. Something clicked and we had tremendous chemistry, so Mark hired us solidly for about four years touring the country together in a variety of different plays, including one starring Father and one directed by him. It was like a touring family unit. Marjorie was my agent for the infamous "blonde era" where I went peroxide. I recall she came to watch the recording of my *Rising Damp* episode, *Hello Young Lovers*.

"Well, what did you think?" I asked as I sat back in the dressing room after the studio session.

"You must be aware of your hair," she replied, straight-faced.

I couldn't believe it.

"You had your hair up at the back," she continued, "and you could see the black roots coming through."

Well there was no way there were any roots showing, the make-up girls would have dealt with that for a start-off. That was all she said; nothing about my performance or the show, just my hair!

The peroxide look had been instigated by my brother-in-law, Christopher Matthews, who lived with Dilys for a long time. He came up to me one day at the Hall and suggested it.

"You ever thought of going blonde?" he asked.

"No," I answered.

"Well you should, you've got the right face for it."

I was out of work and thought it couldn't hurt to try, so I went for it. And it worked as far as getting more jobs was concerned! I elected, however, not to take his other advice, which was to get a nose job. Daddy always called it my "fly slide", but there was absolutely no way I was going to go under the knife. Hair colour is one thing; surgery is completely different. The blonde came to an end one day when I attempted some root touch-up on my own. The black turned purple and I decided it would be far easier to go back to my natural colour. Besides, I don't think that gentlemen necessarily prefer blondes...

Which makes it all the more ironic that I made my pantomime debut in *Goldilocks and the Three Bears*. I had changed agents to a chap called Kenny Earl and he was big on the variety side of the business. I had never done pantomime before and was very sceptical about doing one, which is funny now when I consider how big a part of my life it has become. I took a lot of persuading from Kenny because I had no interest in all the singing, dancing and audience participation. But eventually he wore me down and I accepted the part of Golidlocks, and was on my way to Stevenage.

Well, I was petrified. Cast alongside me was one Colin Baker, albeit before he had appeared in *Doctor Who*. This being 1980 he was better known for his villainous character as Paul Merroney in *The Brothers*, so in true panto style he was Heinkel, the evil ringmaster who kidnapped my poor bears! Colin was dressed all in black leather and carrying a whip, and being a mischievous fellow used to threaten all manner of misdemeanours with it. My then husband, Nick Field, was in it as one of the broker's men, and it was directed by Chris Moreneo.

My initial fears were soon overcome and I began to love doing it. The audience interraction was wonderful; you have to ad-lib like mad, so it keeps you on your toes. If someone shouts out something you have to keep topping them. I remember that happening once when I was playing the title role in *Cinderella* at the Theatre Royal in Nottingham with Roy Hudd as Buttons. Towards the end of the play the audience said something to him, he said something back for the laugh and I topped it, quite off the cuff, to even greater laughter. Roy was put out. He came over to me after we'd got off stage.

"Well, what happened tonight won't always happen... I mean tonight was, different?" he said.

"How do you mean, different?" I asked.

"Well, the audience were on your side all night," he continued.

"Oh yes they were," I smiled. "And wasn't it wonderful?"

Roy was a lovely man to work with and put a great deal of enthusiasm into the production. He came to me one day and said:

"The scene in the kitchen, it's really not working, is it?"

"No," I agreed, "it's lacking something."

We hadn't opened at this point, so we were still able to make changes.

"Well let me think about it overnight," he concluded, "and I'll see what I can come up with."

Well, he arrived the next morning with a very ambitious number involving Cinders on the kitchen table pretending it was a carriage and lots of dancing and singing, which was brilliant. But when were we going to rehearse and put it in?

"Tonight," he smiled, "preview night!"

I thought he was mad. But we did it. And it worked really well. The preview night was dedicated to the underprivileged children of Nottingham who were given free tickets to come and see us as a treat. I remember they all carried lamps through the streets on their journey to the theatre from different parts of the city, and I could see this beautiful sight out of my dressing room window that evening. The children seemed to empathise with poor Cinders and how oppressed she was by her ugly sisters. This came to a head when Bernard Bresslaw, who was playing one of the sisters, had to hit me hard and send me flying backwards over the dressing table. Well, he hit me, over I flew... and the audience went into an uproar!

"You BASTARD!" screamed the kids. "Don't you bloody hit her!"

The language was atrocious, so I had to get up, walk to the front of the stage and put my hands up for silence.

"It's okay, I am all right, calm down now," I shouted.

The audience went silent.

One lone voice piped up in the dark.

"If you do that to her again, I'll bloody well fix you!"

Chapter Six

Sometimes events off stage can be just as dramatic, if not more so, than those on it. This was to be conclusively proven during the final week of my tour in *Little Women* in 1974. We were at the Grand Theatre, Wolverhampton during a matinee when a sound started to blare out, completely unexpectedly. It had the shrill metal screech of a fire alarm, and the safety curtain was dropped halfway through a scene, separating ourselves from the audience. It was a bomb scare. Everyone was evacuated onto the pavement outside; it was quite a picture with the public clutching their coats and looking round in confusion, and the cast in their period costumes doing much the same. It transpired that it was a false alarm, so we were able to return to the theatre and resume the performance.

Things got a darn sight hairier, however, later that week during another performance. I was playing Beth, and had a scene with the actress playing Jo, Susan Wooldridge. There were just the two of us on the stage when this voice boomed out of the darkness.

"I am an American citizen and I do not agree with the politics of this play."

Susan and I exchanged glances. Clearly the chap was unhinged; best just to continue and ignore it.

"I do not agree with the politics of this play," he repeated, adding resonance to his voice. "And I have a gun."

Susan's eyes widened and she looked at me in pure terror.

"Carry on with the dialogue," I whispered, "but start moving very slowly off the stage."

The American man was still shouting his threats from the darkness. We couldn't see him, but we could hear him. And we could hear his threats.

Susan was a much taller and broader girl than I, but she was getting steadily paler and beginning to tremble. Gently, but surely, I ushered her towards the safety of the wing. The whole thing can't have lasted more than two minutes in total, but it felt like an eternity for the two of us up on that stage. I was amazed Susan didn't faint; the colour had drained from her body completely by the time we got backstage. The police apprehended the man, who didn't have a gun at all. Not that we could have possibly known. The whole incident highlighted just how exposed one is on the stage, and certainly brought the tour to a very unsettled conclusion.

That in itself was a shame because I had had great fun touring with it, and become a kind of matriarchal figure to the other girls in the cast. Playing Beth on stage had translated into our everyday lives and I sort of mothered Susan and Stacy Dorning, who was best known from *Black Beauty*. Actress Honor Shepherd, who was a theatrical mother to say the least, was Stacy Dorning's mother and would always slap a thick layer of lipstick onto her daughter, which looked hideous, so whenever she was away I would tell Stacy to take it off because she didn't need it. The other sister was played by Penny Croft, daughter of the comedy writer David. I looked out for the girls, listened to their problems, and gave them reassurance.

One of the benefits of touring is the variety, and often varying quality, of digs. When we were performing *Little Women* in Bath we had quite a surprise at breakfast. We had been pre-booked in the night before and not met the proprietors, so imagine the shock when we were served our bacon and eggs by a fabulous vision in a gold lamé halterneck top and lycra hotpants! Stacy's eyes nearly popped out of her head because she quickly realised it was a man! The hotel was run by two gay guys who had a club in the basement. A couple of times we went back there after the show; and Hamish, my love interest on and off stage at the time, took me dancing one night. They had a band on playing a few songs, so everyone started to let their hair down a bit. Halfway through a song a young lady interceded.

"My turn now mate," she said, sliding her arm round my back and starting to move closer.

It was a very strange situation. I don't mind a bit of attention, but this woman was starting to get, shall we say, quite amorous. She started to push closer and her arm locked tighter around me.

"Are you from round here?" I asked, trying in vain to attempt conversation.

She was a short step away from intimate, so when the song finished I made my farewells and headed to the loos. The toilets were located right the way across the room and at the top of a staircase. So imagine my complete shock when I got to the top of the stairs and the girl was standing there waiting for me. She couldn't possibly have got there ahead of me! I kept seeing this same girl throughout the night in different places and couldn't get my head around how she was moving about so fast. It transpired that they were twins who were both vying for my affections and having a little tease at the same time. We all saw the funny side of it in the end!

❧

A little warmer than Bath, my next job saw me head out to the Mediterranean, to Malta, where I was to perform and direct for a season. My agent was called up by Carl Coupet Management one day.

"I know Debbie's done *Girl in My Soup*, but how would she like to come out to Malta to star in it and direct it?" he asked.

"There's another play by Francis Durbridge called *Suddenly at Home* for her too."

I agreed and, after two weeks of rehearsal in London, was soon packed off to work at a beautiful little theatre in the capital city of Valetta. Carl had sadly not got anything organised for my arrival. There were no props, so I was forced to go out round the shops and cafes to beg, steal and borrow everything. The stage management team only had one member who could speak English, who was sadly not the lighting guy. I was forced to develop a strange ritualistic sign language with him to enable us to achieve what I wanted. For instance, I'd mime covering my eyes and shading my face to get a darker lighting effect, or do jazz hands and arc my hands like the sun to get it brighter. It was all very basic, but I liked the challenge.

The Maltese love their theatre. The seating was a tiered system of boxes rather than seats, and on the first night of *Girl in My Soup* I was astounded to see the rather incongruous sight of people dressed up in all their evening finery. Gold and diamonds glittering, full-length frocks for the ladies, dinner suits for the gentlemen; there was a real sense of occasion to it, which you don't really get in this country. At the end of the performance we got a standing ovation. I adored performing over there, and the lifestyle during the day. All the little bars and patisseries; I became quite enchanted with the ways of the Mediterranean!

When I got back to the UK I did a play called *Same Time Next Year* by Bernard Slade. It's about a couple who are married to different people, and have an affair. They meet up once a year for a few days, and no more; hence the play's title. It charted the course of these two people for near enough the whole of their lives. I remember having to play from 18 to 65, via some very rapid costume changes. Literally we had seconds in the wings to get ready for the next scene; no time to get shy about stripping off.

The other lead in *Same Time* was Norman Eshley, who was best known for playing the neighbour in the sitcom *George and Mildred*, and the play was directed by Sebastian Graham Jones. We were a very close-knit group, the three of us, as it was a two-hander with no other cast members. We rehearsed in London, and opened in Guildford. The first scene of the play started with the pair of us in bed together, and for it to look authentic I was completely naked underneath the duvet. I then had to pull the duvet around my body and walk across stage left to get a glass of water. A very simple action. On the opening night, however, Norman followed too closely behind me; his foot caught the tail end of the duvet and I was unveiled in my full glory to the audience. It got a round of applause!

The most pressing thing at the time, I recall, was that both men were vying for my attention. I went for Norman, who turned out to be completely the wrong choice. Norman had been married to Millicent Martin for a while, but they had long since divorced. Anyway, we dated for a while, but things didn't work out and we split up, whilst still doing the play. This meant we had the delicate problem of being an ex-couple in real life playing a couple having a passionate affair on stage, but we were professional and coped with it.

The seeds of the ending of our relationship were sown one day when there was a knock at the door of my flat in Wandsworth. I answered, and there was Nick Field, whom I had split up with to start dating Norman. He looked a broken man. He was thin, tired and white as a sheet. He'd popped round to bring me an Easter egg, so I thanked him and he went on his way. As I shut the door I turned round and looked at Norman.

"I can't do this to him," I said. "He's in a terrible state, he just can't cope."

A little while later we had a break in touring, and I took Norman to one side. We were no longer together at this point.

"I've decided to marry Nick," I told him.

"Yes, I rather thought you would," he answered. "Well I've got a lady who's a make-up artist at Yorkshire Television and I'm going to marry her."

I was a little taken aback, having considered how best to tell him what I was doing, only to be trumped by that revelation. Well! Anyway, we both got married, then two weeks later were back on the road together, only this time he was married and I was married. It was all rather peculiar.

෪

In the early seventies I was up for the part of Georgina in the series *Upstairs Downstairs*. Having beaten Lesley Ann Down to the lead role in *Take Me High*, it was time for our fortunes to be reversed, and she got the part. A few years later the same team were casting for a new drama about a bomb disposal team, *Danger UXB*. The producer of the series, John Hawkesworth, called me up and asked me to go along to meet him at Euston Films, which was situated on Clapham Common. I had my own flat on Wandsworth Common, so it wasn't too far to go. I went over and there was John, along with a selection of the directors they were going to use. I was at the height of my "blonde period", and John told me how lovely it was to see me again. I read for them, and when I had finished John looked up at me.

"I think I owe you one, don't I?"

"Yes, I think you do."

"Right, you've got the part," he smiled. "You're Naughty Norma!"

It was another couple of months before filming started, so I took the role in *There's a Girl in My Soup* opposite Frederick Jaeger, but the tour was extended and I ended up filming *UXB* during the day, then having to travel to the theatre to do *Girl* in the evening. It was absolutely exhausting.

I was also concerned as to how I should approach playing Norma.

"What about her character then, John?" I asked.

"Well she's an East End girl, a cockney," he began.

"Yes," I said, hoping for something more concrete.

"She's a sort of mix between Marilyn Monroe and Diana Dors with a Clapham accent," he concluded.

Norma was a very flirtatious young madam and a total joy to play. She was very sexually turned on, especially when the bombs started falling. She wouldn't go down into the air raid shelter, she would leap on the nearest soldier for a quicky. My first scene was shot on location. It was all 1940s gear, and the dress I wore was a very close fitting blue number, out over the boobs and nipped in at the waist. I had the big Diana Dors hairdo and thick red lipstick; a total transformation. My make-up ladies on this, coincidentally, were also the same ones who had made me up for *That'll Be the Day*. At the end of the recording John called me in to watch the rushes; I was so nervous, I just hoped I'd got it right. We all packed in, and there was this vision on screen: Norma. I didn't recognise her as me, it was such a shock! I also felt a sense of glowing pride, which is rare when one watches one's own work. John, however, said nothing, and kept stony-faced throughout. This began to unnerve me. The rushes finished, the lights went up, and I plucked up the courage to speak.

"Well, what did you think?" I asked, my mouth going dry.

He put his hand on mine and looked at me.

"You've got *her* exactly right," he said, emphasising the "her".

"What do you mean 'her'?" I replied, puzzled.

"I based that character on my first girlfriend during the war, and you've done it spot on."

I absolutely adored playing Norma, it was such a fun feisty part. One great compliment I was paid was that the prop boys used to watch me record my scenes. Ordinarily they would disappear for a fag until they were required to redress the set, but they always hung about to follow me. On occasion, I even used to get a round of applause!

Norma had a major fetish for air raids. To put it simply, the bombing turned her on. Anthony Andrews, who had played opposite me in *Take Me High*, starred as one of the soldiers Norma took it upon herself to try and seduce during the Blitz. We did a long scene together where I had to leap on him and try to undress him. We managed it in one take; and then there was a cutaway of me at the end of a long corridor, dressed only in a dressing gown. Anthony had to walk down the corridor towards me and then I dropped my gown to reveal all. Unfortunately the two sound guys sat behind me hadn't realised quite how much was going to be unveiled, and dropped the boom straight into shot as I bared all.

"I'm sorry, I'm so sorry," gushed the one. "I didn't realise we were going to see your boobs!"

Red-faced, he repeated himself.

"I didn't realise we were going to see your boobs!"

So I had to do it all over again!

≈

My boobs were quite a heavy feature of the publicity for the series. Looking through cuttings at the time, there are a fair few playing on the sexy image Norma had, like GIRL ON A LONG FUSE or DANGER – BLONDE BOMBSHELL!, but the most comical has to be DEBBIE... UX BOOBS! It is so of its time.

The fact that Norma was such a saucy character added well to this line of media exposure, and a photocall was set up with myself and a platoon of soldiers. It was at an airbase in Yorkshire, and the boys had just come back from Northern Ireland. I was appearing in a play in Harrogate, so it was organised that I would become the unit mascot. These things come back to haunt you when you least expect it, and a few months ago my website designer David received an email from the soldier who was stood next to me in the photograph. He had a copy of the original and wanted to send it through for me to sign. Of course I complied, and he sent me through a very nice letter, and it turns out that he's now a grandfather... something which is quite frightening when I can still clearly remember the day we did the photo! Thirty years have passed; it's quite extraordinary.

That was quite a nice piece of publicity, but the worst I ever got involved in was for a play called *The Sack Race*. There was a photo shoot with myself and a monkey – rather unamusingly also called Debbie – to promote the play, which was running at the Theatre Royal in Newcastle prior to a stint in the West End. The monkey was an evil little creature and leapt onto my shoulder, tearing out a chunk of my hair by the roots. I was in agony and had to be extra careful arranging my hair so as not to show off the bald patch for weeks after. This was compounded by the press thinking it would be funny to reunite me with my monkey namesake for another photo in my dressing room. Like a fool I agreed. This time everything was going fine until it caught a glimpse of its own reflection in the mirror. It freaked out, jumped at the mirror, shattering it and spraying shards of glass everywhere, before having another try for another chunk of my hair! I can safely say that I have avoided contact with monkeys ever since.

At the end of the series Norma was made an honest lady – well, as honest as she was ever going to get – as she got married. I was appearing in *There's a Girl in My Soup* at Windsor at the same time, which meant I was up at five in the morning to film all day on *UXB*, and would then drive over to the theatre for the evening performance and wouldn't make it home until midnight. It was a punishing schedule, and I was so tired I used to sleep between takes. I literally used to lie on the floor in my wedding dress and have a quick snooze, then snap awake and film whichever scene we were recording at the time.

Tim Wilson was my agent during *UXB*. It was a large agency with bases in London and America, so there was always the option of looking for job opportunities in the States. But I never took it up. To my mind it didn't make sense, while I was doing well in England, to just up sticks and move over there to chase parts. If something had come up I would have looked at it. Father was actually offered a big contract in America early on in his career, but his great friend at the time persuaded him not to. He said it would be far better for him to do the stage classics in Britain, rather than doing movies in Hollywood. So he said no to a multi-film deal with Warner Brothers, which is a great shame as he certainly had the matinee idol looks and the acting ability to have made a big impact over there.

Chapter Seven

In 1977 I took a role in the J.B. Priestley play *Laburnum Grove*, with Arthur Lowe and his wife Joan Cooper. They had met years previously in rep when Joan had been the leading lady and Arthur had joined the company. In fact my mother had shared a flat with Joan when she was in rep in Colchester. The couple married and had children, and of course Arthur's career took off and he was hugely successful, most famously as Captain Mainwaring in *Dad's Army*.

In later life they decided they wanted to work together as much as possible, which meant that Arthur would inevitably get cast in different roles and then proceed to try anything he possibly could to secure his wife a part in the same production. On this occasion the pair of them were playing my parents, and Stacy Dorning's mother, Honor Shepherd, was playing my aunt. It was a very long tour, but an enjoyable one.

Arthur and Joan both liked their booze. One night whilst we were appearing in Bath, they asked me to escort them back to their hotel. They got to stay in a hotel, whereas I, being further down the billing, was in far more humble digs. I agreed and had Arthur on one arm and Joan on the other. I started to walk them back to the hotel, both completely gone. I mean, they were swaying about all over the place, with little me stuck in the middle trying to keep them upright. Arthur was a small round fellow and proved particularly troublesome to keep on his feet! I was saved any further embarrassment by the generosity of the hotel's doorman, who took on the tipsy duo and we bade each other goodnight.

Duncan Wheldon, who was producing the play, announced that we were going into the West End. But there was to be a sting in the tail. He took Arthur to one side and told him gently: "We're going to do it on one proviso: we recast your wife, she just isn't good enough." I sadly have to agree with him – she wasn't. She could barely walk across the stage, more a sort of shuffle; and her voice didn't project into the audience, it was muffled. Arthur was torn apart over it. He was loyal and devoted to his wife and just couldn't face being in a situation where he had to choose the production over his wife and her feelings. I only knew all of this was going on because Arthur confided in me. I had grown close to the pair, so much so that I had become like a sort of second daughter to them.

Eventually Arthur talked them round into keeping Joan in the production. And so we opened at the Duke of York's Theatre, my name up in lights; it was too good to be true. Opening night came and I got to meet J.B. Priestley, who was a legend. Mother and Father came to the opening night; Father had appeared in Priestley's *Time and the Conways* many years before. Priestley welcomed him with a "hello young boy", and we all laughed a lot; there was no way Daddy was a young boy any more! We got good notices; well, nearly all of us. The news swept round like wildfire that you had to go and see *Laburnum Grove* at the Duke of York's to see the most dreadful performance in the whole of the West End. It became quite the thing, albeit in such a cruel sense. We stayed open for a couple of months, but I fear our fate was sealed from the outset.

Derek Nimmo was my co-star in the 1978 production of *A Little Bit of Fluff*, in which I played Mamie Scott, alongside

Damaris Hayman. It was a period farce and my role had been played on film many years previously by Betty Balfour. Derek and I got along with each other very well, until one night when we had a slight mishap on stage. His character was meant to get rid of me very quickly by dragging me across the stage, flinging me through a door into the bedroom and then slamming it shut. Easy, you would think.

"Quick, no one must see you," he panicked as he pushed me through the door.

Slam. Only it wasn't the gentle slam required, it was a real thump. I pushed my hands onto it and realised it wasn't moving; it had slammed shut permanently. I forced all my (admittedly minimal) weight against it, but nothing. I was trapped off stage. My cue was approaching rapidly, and I looked around for inspiration. There was a balcony on the back of the set. It would be a scramble, but I could just make it before I was due on. So I did. In my full flowing period gown I heaved myself up and over the balcony, landing on stage behind Derek who was expecting me to reappear from the bedroom at any moment. I walked up behind, tapped him on the shoulder and gave him the fright of his life!

Derek was an unusual man in some ways; perhaps a little over-boisterous. He seemed to have no concept of his own physical strength, so what to him seemed like a little tap or a push actually carried some considerable force. I remember he gave me an affectionate punch on the arm whilst we were waiting in the wings one night, and the force actually threw me over onto the floor.

In the late seventies and eighties I did a lot more theatre than I did television. Amongst the television work I did was a Brian Rix pilot for the BBC, on which I had the same wardrobe lady as I'd had on *Doctor Who*, my dear friend Linda. I don't remember very much about it at all, except that I was very nervous about doing it because I hadn't done any television in a while. Brian, of course, was renowned for dropping his trousers in farces for cheap laughs in the West End, but this pilot didn't come together at all well. I believe there was only ever one series made: it was pretty awful!

Accident on the other hand was a nice little cameo part for me. It was only one scene, opposite Bernard Kay, where I played a manipulative little madam who was ripping off all his money. I worried at the time that I might have overacted somewhat; indeed when Dougie Camfield (who directed me not long after on *Danger UXB*) saw it, he told me he thought I was over the top. But on reflection I don't think I was too bad. There's always a worry when you move from stage to television that you might use the wrong style of acting; television needs to be pulled right back because everything is told in close-up, whereas on stage things need to be overstated a little more because the audience is further away, and you need to project your voice to the back wall.

On the day we recorded this there was a delay in studio, which meant the scene was pushed back. The longer one has to wait around on a shoot, the more nervous one becomes; so by the time it came round to shooting my bit I was a jibbering wreck, quite honestly. It was a long scene, and quite involved, with various movements to remember and different camera cues to pick up. I walked on, said a couple of lines, then fluffed; that was how nervous I was. But the director was very kind and let me carry on, then we did a retake straight after. I was fine on the second take; it had just been the build-up from all the waiting around I'd done that day.

In hindsight I think I should have done less theatre than I did, and pursued more television roles. On the one hand it's down to what jobs came along, but on the other I think maybe it would have helped me more to do more TV work. The trouble was that there came the point where I wasn't quite young enough to be the sweet and innocent girl next door, and not old enough for the mature character parts one gets later on in life. Men are always very well catered for in the industry, but the parts do lack for the ladies. Not that it's always a matter of taking the better parts; acting is still a job regardless, and you have to pay the mortgage just the same as anyone else. I've done some terrible productions. I did some atrocious ones with dear Henry McGee. But then you get something brilliant like *Same Time Next Year* or *Wife Begins at Forty*, and your faith is restored.

I never ventured much into the world of radio during my career, mainly because I wasn't keen on reading live scripts; it could be something to do with my dyslexia, but I prefer to study a script over and over, and virtually learn it all off by heart. But I was cast as a regular in the BBC radio series *Tony's*. It starred Victor Spinetti and John Laurie, and was set in a hairdressing salon. It still gets repeated on BBC Radio 7 to this day, such is the way these things are recycled. I was Maisy the cockney trainee hairdresser, and we made about seven episodes. It was all recorded at the Palace Theatre in Regent Street in front of a live audience; we would line up to do it, and they put me on a box so I could reach my microphone. I liked doing it in front of an audience; you get a real buzz from the laughs coming back, and get a better sense of the rhythm and timing.

We were recording one day, and I was stood next to John at the mic, and I could see him start to falter. He then collapsed to the floor in agony, clutching his chest. Everything stopped, and an ambulance was called; he had suffered a heart attack, a near fatal one, and sadly he died not long afterwards.

Having got along with Arthur Lowe so well whilst working on *Laburnum Grove*, I was pleased to hear that he wanted to work with me once more on a new production. It was called *Beyond a Joke* and, of course, co-starred his wife Joan Cooper. There was a great part for a young male lead with lots of physical comedy which I thought would be right for my husband, Nick Field, so I suggested him. They agreed, and so it came about that we were two husband-and-wife partnerships working together. Nick worked really well in the role; comedy was his forte, it was drama where he fell down. He was embarrassing to watch in a straight role, in fact. I suspect he had inherited a lot of his comedic skills from his father, Sid Field; but he used to feel under the shadow of his father, and couldn't quite live up to him, or his reputation, which was a great shame really.

Arthur used to have a wooden-hulled boat – one of the oldest in England, if not the world – and wherever possible he would moor it close to the venues we played. His son used to travel with them and skipper the boat, and they would use it as accommodation when it was near enough. We had a rather wonderful dinner on board one night, along with his son Steven, whom I never took to, and his lady friend who was bizarrely known as "Mr Bear". I couldn't tell you why. It was a very unusual set-up.

Birthday Suite with Brian Murphy and Trevor Bannister came along a couple of years later. I'd done a two hander with Trevor called *Your Place or Mine* in the late seventies, so we knew each other quite well. Trevor always rather resented his association with *Are You Being Served?* It had been a smash hit in the seventies, and he told me that it was originally written for him as the lead. However, once John Inman came in as Mr Humphries, Trevor felt that he became somewhat sidelined. As a result he carried quite a chip on his shoulder.

He was also rather aggressive on stage. When we did a play at the Jersey Opera House together, we shared a scene with Barbara Windsor, and Babs would literally use me as a shield and hide behind my back. He had no control of his own strength. In *Birthday Suite* he slammed the door too erratically and managed to draw blood from the poor lad playing the juvenile lead.

We liked each other, and worked well on stage. But there was always something a little unusual about him which I couldn't quite put my finger on. He didn't tolerate fools. In fact he didn't tolerate actors either. As a result he kept himself to himself, and when he did talk he didn't have a pleasant word to say about anyone else.

I seem to have done a disproportionate number of theatre productions with Trevor, now I come to think of it. We worked together again in 1998 on *Funny Money*, alongside Henry McGee and Rodney Bewes. Ron Alridge was the director, and it was a farce written by Ray Cooney. The first day of rehearsals came and we all gathered together in a large room, seated in a circle: the director, the writer and the entire cast all ready to read it through together. I was sat next to Rodney, as I was playing his wife. Of course nobody learns the lines before a readthrough, that's the whole point of it. But we'd only been going a few minutes when Rodney shut his script and threw it onto the floor.

"Don't worry, I know this," he announced.

"You what?" I said, surprised.

"I know it," he replied calmly.

Know it? He didn't have a clue, he knew none of it. He indignantly refused to pick up the script, which meant nobody quite understood what was going on. Ray found it terribly amusing and we managed to make it through.

Rodney was a quirky fellow. Just before the curtain was due to go up the call would sound out: "Beginners please: Miss Watling, Mr Bewes." I would be in the wings stage left, he would be stage right. All of a sudden he would go out into the centre stage, fall to his knees, clasp his hands together in a praying position and lean forward so the points of his fingers touched the stage, then straighten up, then duck back down again. Then he would pull himself up and get back to his starting position. It was curious to say the least. Every performance without fail he would follow this very individual ritual.

The first night, however, was a complete nightmare. It was, I recall, at the Theatre Royal in Windsor. Sorry as I am to say this, Rodney had not learnt it properly, and was feeding me bum lines all night. I had to carry the first half, which was not a pleasant situation. He didn't seem to know which scene he was in, and I certainly couldn't tell. I didn't recognise any of his lines; it was definitely not from the script everyone else had read. The worst part was that he thought he'd done so well!

In the interval Henry and the director Ron came into my dressing room to see me.

"Thank goodness it was you on stage," said Ron gratefully.

"I couldn't understand what he was doing," added Henry.

"You saved us out there," concluded Ron.

The trouble was, in order for the piece to make sense, whilst Rodney was making up all kinds of nonsense, I was having to say his lines for him as well as saying my own, in effect doubling my part. Not only that, but I had to rephrase them so that it made sense that my character was saying them; all that off the cuff too! Ron's next port of call was Rodney's dressing room.

"Didn't that go well?" chirped Rodney, reaching for a drink, as Ron entered.

Ron picked him up by the scruff of his neck and pushed him against the wall.

"Don't you ever, ever do that again," he growled. "Learn your lines, Rodney, or else."

He made it through the second act, but he looked like a quivering wreck. Not surprising given what had just happened backstage. To give him his due, he did improve as we went on, although he was still quite mad. It was a very eventful first night for what was to be a very long tour. We literally played everywhere, up and down the country.

Corpsing is something one tries to avoid at all costs on stage. There was one night during the run of *Funny Money* where Henry McGee came walking on stage and took an almighty tumble down behind the sofa. Obviously we were all wondering if he was okay, whilst at the same time trying to remain calm and continue with the play. Dear Anita Graham, who was a delightfully potty lady, roared with laughter. She was bending over clutching her stomach, with tears rolling down her face. Of course once she'd started, we all started; and to add to it Henry slowly raised his head back up from behind the sofa, before pulling it back down again for comedy effect. I mean you should absolutely never do that in a play, but with *Funny Money* we got away with it several times because the audience would join in with the laughter. I had great fun doing the play, and had to pretend to be drunk for the whole of the second act… I liked that!

In 1986 I did a play called *Rattle of a Simple Man*. It's a two-hander, and I played a hooker who picks up a football fan and then takes him back to her place. The big question was: who could we get to play the other part? We deliberated over several names, and it was my husband Steve who suggested my brother-in-law Seymour. It was a short tour, and we opened in Preston, where the management were terrible. Henry Sherwood, who had run a production company with Father years ago, and was very dapper and well turned out, wanted to put on *Rattle* as a way of getting back into the business. However, in the passing years he had lost all of his money and when I went to meet him he looked like a down-and-out. When we arrived in Preston for our dress rehearsal I was horrified at how basic the set was. It looked dreadful. So, just like I did in Malta, I set about modifying and finishing off the set myself. The trouble was this was the day we opened!

"How lovely to have my leading lady dressing the set," laughed Henry.

"I'm having to do it," I said with a steely stare, "because it looks so darned awful!"

I managed to find time to put my costume on for the first time only twenty minutes before curtain up.

It was a terrible tour and one I shall never forget, even though it was only three weeks long. We played Malvern, where Mother and Father came to offer their support, and we stopped in digs called Poet's Retreat. I certainly couldn't imagine anything other than rats retreating to these lodgings: they were utterly horrific. I was certainly not sad to see the back of *Rattle*, although it had been great working with

Seymour. We went on to work together a few more times in various productions such as *Spring and Port Wine*, and it has always been a pleasure.

Chapter Eight

Nick Field was my first husband, and I came to meet him, as you'd expect, through an acting job. I was on the road with Henry McGee doing a show called *She Won't Lie Down*, which was directed by my father. He asked if I would like to sit in on auditions for the part of the young lover, which I did; and in walked this handsome young man, Nick Field. Nicola, my sister, was working on the production too as assistant stage manager, or ASM, and it wasn't long before the two of them became an item. He was her first proper boyfriend, and after the play finished they kept seeing each other, and he would come to visit the Hall. Nick soon very firmly became a part of the family. He could be terribly camp in many ways, and his sense of humour had us all in stitches.

After about three years together, Nicky ended the relationship with him. I remember Nick was terribly distraught because he wasn't just losing a girlfriend, he thought he was losing the whole family. In particular he looked upon my father as if he were his own. Nick and Nicky had even done a couple of seasons together at the Frinton summer theatre. However, things hadn't worked out between him and my sister; but the split sent him into a downward spiral, and he began to have a kind of breakdown. He would come to the Hall week after week, even when Nicky wasn't there, and it was quite some time before he pulled himself back together.

One day, quite out of the blue, the phone rang at my flat in Wandsworth.

"Hello Debs, it's Nick," he said.

I was pleased to hear from him and glad that he was feeling better.

"Look, we've always been close, like brother and sister, and it would be a shame to stop seeing each other, so would you like to come out for an Indian one evening?" he asked.

He was living in Putney, which was nearby, and I could see no reason why not, and agreed. We argued for a little while about which one of us knew the better restaurant, but eventually settled on a venue and date. It was just like old times, and we laughed and joked as if nothing had changed. At the end of the evening he walked me home.

"Well, thank you for a lovely night, but I've got to be up early in the morning," I said, reaching into my bag for my keys. "I'll see you very soon."

I turned the key in the lock and turned back to look at him. Our eyes met and something clicked. A spark: something new I had never seen in him before. Nick later told me that he had driven round London for hours afterwards because he'd had the same reaction, like an electric shock. We'd known each other for so long, but never ever considered ourselves as being anything more than strictly platonic. However, from that moment on things were going to change.

It soon became time for me to take Nick to the Hall as my fella. That was tricky, to say the least. Mother and Father were very pleased to see him again; Nicky less so, understandably I guess given the situation, but she did not take it very well at all. Nicky was with Seymour by this point, who was to become her husband, so it wasn't simply a question of being jealous. I remember having my hen party at the Hall; everybody dressed up, sitting around the long spotlessly varnished dining table, laughing and drinking. Nicky was seated on my left.

"Don't do it," she said, placing her hand firmly on my forearm. "You don't know what you're letting yourself in for."

Her eyes were slightly teary against all the joviality surrounding us. I placed my hand on top of hers.

"It's my decision," I said calmly.

"Don't do it, I promise you he's not worth it," she implored. "Do not do this."

I ignored her advice, and went through with it.

Everything was fine for quite some time. We moved into a house in Teddington, but things began to crumble because Nick hadn't quite got to grips with the fact that I was, to all intents and purposes, a woman of independent means. He was expecting, I think, for me to be the wife and for him to be the provider and to pay all the bills. In reality my career was far more successful than his, and he began to get jealous; and that jealousy began to eat him from the inside like a cancer. He started to question, "Why is she getting these parts?" – which was completely ridiculous, because it wasn't as if we were going up for the same roles.

Nick got a summer season at the Theatre Royal in Jersey at the same time as I was touring as the lead role in *Gigi*, in a production with Ralph Bates. Nick and I both knew our relationship was on the rocks, but neither of us was prepared to admit it. Nick was sharing digs with a young man called Steve Turner. Steve would later become my second husband; he was the bass player in a band playing at a nightclub called Caesar's Palace, where they had dancers and singers in a big vaudeville-style show. Well, I was doing my thing over here, and Nick was doing his own thing over there, when one day a huge bouquet of flowers arrived at the theatre. I was sitting looking at them when Ralph walked in.

"Who are those from?" he asked.

"Nick," I replied.

"Oh dear, what's he been up to?" he said, shaking his head.

I looked up at him.

"I really don't know any more," I answered.

I finished the *Gigi* tour, having had a thoroughly wonderful time with Ralph who was a lovely man, and decided it was time to head out to Jersey. I had to try and see if I could save our marriage. I told Nick I was coming, and took the next available flight.

It was Sunday morning, I remember it distinctly. I got off the plane with my hand luggage in one hand and the Sunday newspapers tucked under my other arm, and walked up the long corridor to collect the rest of my cases. All of a sudden a young man stepped out in front of me, with two ladies behind him.

"Excuse me, are you Deborah Watling?" he asked.

"Yes," I answered cautiously.

"Well, I'm Steven Turner and this is my girlfriend who's also called Deborah," he explained.

"Okay, but where's Nick?"

"Ah well," he said taking a deep breath. Pause. "They'll probably be letting him out tomorrow morning."

"WHAT?!" I exclaimed, dropping my newspapers onto the floor. Thoughts starting dashing through my mind, and I began to feel my blood boiling. This was really too much; I decided to get straight back onto the plane and go home. I took a few deep breaths and went over to collect my suitcase. Without warning I was grabbed from behind and hoisted up into the air. It was Nick. He and Steve had decided it would be funny to play a prank on me. I was not amused. At all. I have a photo from my visit to Jersey, of the three of us together; Deborah Watling and her two husbands. Steve often remarks that I'm the only woman he can think of who would have a picture like that!

By coincidence, the following year I was offered a summer season in Jersey at the Opera House, with Barbara Windsor and Trevor Bannister. Dick Ray ran the Opera House as well as Caesar's Palace nightclub, which meant that the cast had to

The House of Watling. From top: Father, Mother, Dilys, Me, Giles, Nicola

TOP LEFT Mother in *A Midsummer Night's Dream* at Regent's Park
TOP RIGHT Nanny, the queen of amdram in Epping
BOTTOM Father with Richard Attenborough in the 1945 film *Journey Together*

As Sally in the 1959 television adaptation of *The Invisible Man*

TOP LEFT Make-up tips from Big Sister
TOP RIGHT Making a guest appearance with Dad in a 1966 episode of *The Power Game*
CENTRE LEFT Filming *Fury from the Deep* (photo copyright © Victor Pemberton)
BOTTOM LEFT Returning to the role of Victoria more than twenty-five years
later in *Downtime* (photo copyright © Robin Pritchard)
BOTTOM RIGHT On location in Snowdonia for *The Abominable Snowmen*

TOP Opening my boutique, The Pink Clock
BOTTOM With Cliff in the poster shot for the 1973 film *Take Me High*

TOP LEFT With Henry McGee in *She Won't Lie Down*
TOP RIGHT With Jack Douglas and Brill "Boysie" Watling-Turner in *Wife Begins at Forty*
BOTTOM Posing on the Great Wall of China on the Far East tour of *A Bedful of Foreigners*

TOP LEFT Cinderella's sad fairy (photo copyright © Ian Burgess)
TOP RIGHT At a *Doctor Who* signing in 2000 (photo copyright © Paul W.T. Ballard)
BOTTOM Taking a break with Mummy after Daddy passed away

The proud Father on my wedding day

be seen in the nightclub to help generate some extra publicity. One night I went along with Babs; we were sitting at a table when I spotted Nick's pretty friend Steve, playing the bass. It turned out he was still part of the resident band. At the end of the set, where he'd done his best Paul McCartney impression, he came up to me and asked if I remembered him. Of course I did! We got together and I thought he'd be a summer season fling… but he followed me back to the mainland. And we're still together, over twenty-five years later. So much for a fling!

I tried my hardest to fight for my first marriage to work; one takes the vows and makes the commitment, so it's hard to see that crumble away. Nick had taken up with another woman, which didn't help; and, whilst appearing in *French Without Tears*, I discovered I was pregnant with his baby. To compound matters further, Nick and myself were contracted to appear in panto together at Reading, in *Aladdin*. I phoned him to tell him that I was pregnant and to ask what we should do. I was in a genuine state of confusion. I hadn't planned to get pregnant, and I was living through the agony of a failed marriage and now having to work with a man I was not on the best of terms with. I'll never know how I made it through that production, not least because "the other woman" was around all the time. She was a pleasant enough lady, but it was rather painful to see the two of them together.

The situation was about as bad as it could get, or so I thought. Nick and I barely spoke, even though there was so much that needed discussing. He hadn't been at all forthcoming about what he thought we should do about the baby. Then, on the last night of the panto, Nick gave me his cold assessment of the situation. He came up to me outside the dressing room and patted my stomach.

"You'll be all right," he said.

Then walked away.

I was completely on my own. And completely broken.

One thing I've always been able to rely upon throughout my life, however, is the strength and support of my family. So,

I packed up my things and returned to Frinton to Mother and Father. I talked things through with them, and we agreed there was no way I could carry on and go through with the pregnancy. They arranged an appointment for me at a clinic in Colchester, where I had an abortion. It was the hardest decision of my life. The doctors there made an error carrying out the operation, and cut me wrongly, which has meant that I've never been able to have a child of my own. Steve and I wanted one so badly; but there was no way it could ever happen, which is so sad, and something I've had to learn to live with.

It was to be many years before I spoke to Nick again.

I was sitting in my bedroom one summer's evening putting on some make-up, getting ready to go out, when the phone rang. Steve was busy sorting out a shirt to wear, so I went downstairs to take the call.

"What the hell are you calling me for?!" I answered in a mixture of shock and anger.

Steve, from upstairs, knew instinctively who was on the other end of the line.

"I'm coming over from LA; I live in LA now, did you know?" Nick said.

"Yes, I know you live in LA," I replied, trying to keep calm.

"Well I'm coming over and I want to see you," he said.

"It's been years Nick, years, what do you want to see me for now?"

"I just want to see you," came the response.

"Well, I see," I said, still somewhat taken off balance. "You'll have to come to the village then, and I'll meet you at the local pub."

There was no way I was going to meet him in my cottage.

"Are you still with Steve?" he asked tentatively.

"Yes, I am. And he happens to be stood right here next to me," I said as Steve put a supportive hand on my shoulder.

"Ah, I see."

"I'll have a word with him," interjected Steve, taking the receiver from my hand. "Hello Nick."

"Hello Steve," came the plaintive answer.

"I shall always be grateful to you, Nick. You did me the biggest favour of my life when you walked out on Debs and I got to be her man."

It had been more than twenty years since I'd last met Nick, and my mind was racing. You don't prepare yourself in your mind for people ageing. I still expected the young Nick from 1981 to be meeting me, but of course he'd grown older and had lived his life since then. I got myself ready and kept thinking what I would say to him and what he would say to me. I was apprehensive at the prospect of meeting him, and made my way unsteadily towards the pub.

I stepped into the pub and glanced round the regulars. Being a small village, everyone knows everyone else, so a few friendly greetings were called out. Then my eyes fixed on a man with a shock of white hair seated on one of the leather sofas. It was Nick. He stood up to greet me, still very thin and tall, with the same almond-coloured eyes. He put his arms round me, hugging me tight and not letting me go. The locals took an intense interest in this, and gave up eating their lunches to see what we were up to. Nick bought me a drink, but it soon became apparent that all eyes were on us and we moved outside to continue our discussion.

Nick had remarried, had two children, and then divorced again. He'd become a househusband and looked after the kids during the week, handing them over to his ex-wife at the weekend.

"Would you come out to LA and meet my daughters?" he asked.

"No, I don't think so," I said, "it's a long way away."

"I'd love you to come and visit," he implored. "You can come and stop in our house and we'll put you up for as long as you like."

"We'll see what happens," I replied tactfully.

He said he'd thought about me a lot over the years, and I guess he wanted what the Americans call "closure". He didn't want to get back together with me or anything like that; but he regretted deeply the way he had treated me all those years ago, such that he just wanted to see me, and I suppose to heal some old wounds. But you can't go back, only forward. He'd moved on since then, and I certainly had. For the better.

We talked on for a while, before I felt it was time to go home. He walked me back down the road to my cottage, and we stood at the gateway.

"Good to see you again, Nick. You take care." I looked at him. "I may see you again."

He lifted me up, held me for a moment, then put me back down again. And then we went our separate ways.

Chapter Nine

A Bedful of Foreigners was a Derek Nimmo production which toured the Far and Middle East. My co-stars included Barry Howard, Jacki Piper and Jeremy Bulloch, but the star name was the legendary Terry Scott. Terry had done this play many, many times and knew exactly what he wanted from everyone and how they should play their parts. I was cast in the role of his wife. The director was Roger Redfarn who had directed me in *Girl in My Soup*. But Terry ruled the roost.

We rehearsed in a church hall in London. Having done my homework, I already knew a large chunk of the play. Barry Howard was playing the waiter and we became great mates during the tour, and still stay in contact to this day. At one point during the tour he pulled on his white suit and took me for a barbecue on the beach and we danced the evening away to the sound of a steel band. Rehearsals couldn't start until Terry arrived. Which he did, eventually. He sat himself down next to me and we began the readthrough.

I was in the middle of a big speech when Terry started to say, "I can't hear her" to Roger. He was sitting next to me, but saying it to the director in a loud voice. It was so rude.

"Excuse me, what?" I said, halting mid-sentence.

Terry looked at me with disdain.

"I can't hear you," he stated.

"Well, you must be deaf."

That didn't set us off on a good footing.

Rehearsals are all about trying things out and getting things wrong so you can improve on them. Having read through, we progressed to blocking some scenes; and, bearing in mind Terry had done this piece a number of times, he had his set ways and timing.

"You're pausing too long," he said.

"You may have done this before, but I haven't," I retorted. "So I'm working it out in my head as we go, is that all right with you?"

"Oh, okay," he said, retreating.

He wasn't used to people answering back. But I was of the mind that if he was going to be difficult, I was going to stand up to him.

A few weeks later we flew out to the Far East, and Terry insisted on a wheelchair at the airport. He was very ill by this point, and on a lot of drugs for his cancer. Having stood up to him at rehearsal, I think he'd forged a grudging respect towards me. We didn't become good friends by any means, but we formed a bond and he gravitated towards me. This meant that he always asked me to push his wheelchair for him. Maybe this was because, with the exception of Jacki, he didn't get along with any of the other cast members. When it got a bit too much for me, dear Jacki would take over sitting with Terry. They of course went back to the *Carry On* days together.

Terry liked his drink, and one day I went down to meet him in the bar. He reached his hand into his pocket and rather protectively pulled out a leather wallet.

"Do you want a drink then?" he asked curtly.

"No thank you, Terry," I replied politely. "You don't buy drinks for anybody. It's your reputation."

"Well I'm doing it now and you might not see it again."

I conceded and let him buy me a drink.

We played hotels on the tour, including the Hilton chain, and performed on stages specially built in their ballrooms. Our crowds were mainly ex-pats and a few locals. It was dinner theatre; the audience would get a posh evening meal, and then afterwards we would perform for them. One night I walked into the wings and Terry was there.

"I've had a terrible day," he frowned.

"Oh dear, have you? Why?"

"I've had all my drugs and I don't feel well at all – I don't think I can perform. So I might walk off and you'll have to carry on without me," he moaned.

Drugs were not the problem. He was drunk. He absolutely reeked of booze.

"OK, Terry," I said. "But if you walk off that stage, I'll be right behind you."

The girl playing the love interest in the play had a terrible time with Terry. Over here she would have been bikini-clad, but it wasn't allowed in the Far and Middle East, so she had a lycra outfit to cover some of her modesty. She was a little bit chunky to play the sex symbol, and Terry was absolutely evil to her. He would even direct her on stage, under his breath, when they were performing. He chipped and chipped away at her until she broke.

"What on earth are you doing to that poor girl?" I said confronting him.

"She's useless, can't do it," he said. "Bloody first job and she's no good."

"Didn't you ever have a first job?" I demanded. "I had a first job, you had a first job. Don't tell me you were brilliant."

During the run we arrived for a few days in Jordan, and the whole cast and crew were invited to a special luncheon by a sheikh. So we duly all gathered in a very luxurious Bedouin tent, with the sheikh at the top of the table. Before we arrived we were warned that under no circumstances should we turn down any food offered to us. It would be seen as discourteous in the extreme.

So out came the first course. Monkey brain. A small brain on a plate, like something we used to look at in biology books at school. I looked round the table at everyone starting to go green. What could I do? I smothered it in salt and pepper, closed my eyes, and swallowed as fast as I could. It couldn't get any worse.

But it did. The second course included snake and fish eyes. With salad, obviously. I breathed in deeply and ploughed on, as everyone around me began to get even more nauseous. I resolved that if anything was brought out on a plate still wriggling, then I would have to concede defeat. I couldn't do that. But I made it through.

Another great experience, while we were playing in Beijing, was visiting the Great Wall of China. It was bloody freezing! I borrowed a jacket to go onto it, and a few of us took a walk along. It snakes up and down and there are little towers at intermittent points which I climbed and from which I admired the breathtaking views. Jeremy Bulloch was the only one who would come up the towers with me, as the others thought they looked decayed and dangerous! I thought to myself that I probably would never come back again, but was very grateful that I had the chance to have a look for myself. The entry points to the Great Wall where you bought the tickets were very touristy. Table upon table of plastic souvenirs, models, tea towels and postcards. There was a real sense of history to China though, never more so than when we visited the palaces. Large, opulent buildings dripping with the riches of so many ancient dynasties; packed with solid gold thrones and intricately carved statues.

❧

Terry managed to get hold of my room number. It was just after twelve when the phone rang.

"Debbie, come to my room, I'm not well," he said in a weak voice.

I was faced with a dilemma. Did I ignore him or go? If I didn't go down to his room and he really was ill, I couldn't stand the guilt of having ignored him. So down I went. I knocked apprehensively on the door and went in. The room was in utter chaos with clothes strewn all over the floor, and there in the middle of the room was Terry in a terrible state. He'd had a turn and was in a real mess. I went and sat next to him on the bed.

"I'm going to have to phone someone to come and clean you up," I said soothingly.

"No, I only want you," he said.

"No Terry, you need proper help."

"I just want a cuddle," he rasped. "Get into bed and cuddle me."

It was sad to see him in this state, but I decided to decline. It wasn't appropriate, and it wasn't going to help him or his condition. He really was a very sad man underneath the stern exterior.

The tour came to an end and we were all saying our goodbyes at the airport.

"Debs, Debs," said Terry, calling me back over. "I've got a book you must read, I'll send it over to you."

"That would be very nice," I smiled.

"But I must have it back," he said, ever the miser. "Understand me? You must send it back to me."

I never thought he would do it. But a few days later a parcel arrived, and true to his word he'd sent me the book. Two weeks later, he died.

Chapter Ten

I was initially very reluctant to get onto the convention circuit. I was well aware that there were lots of events up and down the country and abroad, and was often invited to go along. But I didn't feel right about doing them, either because it wasn't something that appealed to me or I was busy working. It was Pat Troughton who talked me round in the end.

"Come on Debs, you've got to get on the circuit," he said. "I've been doing them in America and it's brilliant out there."

"No, no, no," I protested. "I can't do it. I can't stand up on stage as Deborah Watling, just me with no script."

"Don't be silly, they'll love you," he said reassuringly. "You can do it."

It surprised me greatly that Pat did them. He was an intensely private man, and shied away from any sort of publicity, even when we were making the series. He hated it. But he kept on at me, and I eventually decided to bite the bullet and make my debut.

The first one was a very small event in Cardiff, in a tiny hall, and there were just three guests: me, Vic Pemberton and David Spenser. I was playing in a show in Swansea, so it wasn't any trouble to get to the venue, and Steve agreed to accompany me. There can't have been any more than twenty-five fans in attendance, so it was a very gentle initiation. It was wonderful to meet the fans, who were all so gracious and polite, and enthusiastic about the show. I soon realised that any fears I'd had were totally ill-founded.

Then I was invited to a convention at the University of London, where they had a theatre with a huge auditorium absolutely packed with fans. One had to enter from the back of the auditorium and walk all the way down a flight of steps through the huge audience to reach the stage. It was very daunting. They began announcing different guest names, and as the fans started to get louder I began to shake with nerves.

"I can't do it," I trembled.

"Of course you can," smiled Steve, giving my hand a reassuring squeeze.

More names rolled out, and I knew that mine was going to be the last one.

"And now we have a very special guest..." began the MC.

My heart started to pound faster.

"...you've not seen her for many years, but she's with us here today," he continued, whipping the crowd into a frenzy. "I would like to introduce the lovely Miss Deborah WATLING!!!"

The whole place erupted. They stamped, they clapped, they shouted out for me; it was utterly manic. They hadn't seen me at a large *Who* event like this before and they were uncontrollable. I felt a surge of panic and considered making a break for it, but Steve very gently directed me towards the stage. I don't know how I made it down the steps; it was all a bit of a blur. But I got up on stage, and started to be interviewed, and discovered I could actually be funny. It surprised me how at ease I was. Of course it helped that Victor and David were there again, sending me up something rotten. I think doing the panels has brought out a more comedic side of my personality, insofar as I take no prisoners when being questioned; or if another interviewee is talking nonsense, I will bat it out to the audience with a wry look or a roll of the eyes.

On one occasion Anneke Wills, who was Polly in the series, came out on stage to be interviewed with me and sat down on the sofa in the lotus position, meditating. I looked at her, looked at the audience and back again, and the place exploded in a mass of laughter. Fans will often say how much they have enjoyed my panels because they like my sense of humour and the off-the-cuff remarks. But I'm also not afraid to have poignant moments, like when I'm asked about Dad, or Pat. So it's a mixture of emotions, but all of it very real and true to me.

Kansas City was the location of my first American convention. A member of the *Doctor Who* production team phoned me up at home and said that they were trying to get hold of me to invite me out there and would it be okay to pass on my phone number? I said yes, and within a matter of weeks my US debut was arranged.

Steve dropped me off at Heathrow Terminal 4, and we had a quick drink before we said our goodbyes. Standing at the bar was a pretty ginger-haired lad who followed me through to the departure lounge a few minutes later. I was sitting minding my own business when he came straight up to me and knelt by my feet.

"Hello," he said.

"Hello," I replied politely.

"You're Deborah Watling," he continued.

"And who are you?" I smiled.

"I'm Mark Strickson."

And so that is how I met Mark. He was in *Who* years after I was, so we'd never worked together, but we clicked very quickly and he escorted me onto the plane and insisted on sitting next to me on the flight. I warned him that he wouldn't want to, because in those days I was a smoker, which was then allowed on planes, but he was adamant. It was one heck of a journey with various flight changes in different states, and took about twenty-four hours.

"Stick we me," he said. "I'll get us there!"

True to his word, he organised everything, making sure we got the right connections with the right luggage. By the end of the epic journey we were great mates.

The Kansas convention was on an even bigger scale than the London one. The actors were all assigned assistants to run any errands and bodyguards to escort them round the hotel. When I arrived a burly man presented himself to me and proceeded to check my requirements for the event.

"Do you have any special dietary requirements?" he questioned, ready to note the answer on a clipboard.

"No, no, I'm not allergic to anything," I said, watching him in fascination.

"Do you require bodily protection?" he continued, with a deadpan look on his face.

"Do you mean a suit of armour?" I laughed.

He did not laugh.

The organisation of the whole thing was on such a large scale, it was quite hard to take in. I had two girls whose job it was to knock on the door of my hotel room and escort me to reception. From there somebody else would take over and lead me backstage in readiness for my interview.

"Look, I'm a big girl, I really can cope on my own," I said to one of the organisers.

"No, you must have someone with you at all times," he answered.

I hated it. It felt so claustrophobic. So I decided, in my rebellious way, to make a break for it, without a minder. I picked my moment and made a move towards the hotel door, and had just put one foot out when a voice called out to me.

"Miss Watling, where are you going?"

I turned and smiled.

"Out for a quick walk, some fresh air," I replied innocently.

"We don't walk in this part of Kansas."

Escape plot foiled.

John Levene was also in attendance, holding court as usual. Although he went on to play Sergeant Benton, when I was in it he did two stories inside a Yeti costume. He's always terribly polite when we meet and says, "You were so friendly and welcoming to me on *Doctor Who*. Even though I didn't have any lines you never looked down on me." So he's fond of me and I'm very pleased about that.

I've done many conventions in America, but sadly one never gets to see much of the city where it's being held. The hotels are always so close to the airport; you get to see the terminal when you land, the taxi, the hotel, then back again. Sometimes, if time permits, your minder will take you out on a tour of the city in their car, but very rarely is there enough time for any real sightseeing.

The early eighties saw the biggest conventions ever. The Americans in particular lavished extraordinary amounts of cash on these huge and splendid events. I came onto the circuit just as things had started to peak a little, but even then I was horrified at how many *Who* celebrities were prepared to take advantage of the generosity of the organisers as much as possible. Many an outrageous minibar bill was run up by actors who shall remain nameless. I was in awe of the size of the conventions I went to at the time, so I don't know how I would have coped with ones of the magnitude described to me by Pat.

Even today, people in my village still get very excited when they hear I'm attending a convention. They will ask what I'm doing at the weekend.

"Oh, I'm doing a *Doctor Who* event in Sheffield," I'll say.

"Ooh!" they smile with glee. "Will there be Daleks?"

All of a sudden they are five years old again, and filled with that childish enthusiasm for the show.

"Bring back pictures!" they say.

One person who doesn't come along to conventions is my husband Steve. He came along to my first two to hold my hand whilst I was finding my feet, but bowed out after we went to one in Liverpool. He drove me up, and we arrived in good time to register at the hotel and have an evening meal with the organisers. Then we retired to our room to unpack and get an early night ready for the next day.

In the early morning Steve awoke.

"I've left something in the car," he said, pulling his clothes on. "I'll just pop out and get it."

The room was a sort of L-shape, with a corridor running along the back. He went down the corridor, opened the door, then I heard him shut it very quickly and come walking back into the room. He had a look of total disbelief.

"What's the matter darling?" I said with a yawn.

"I'm not going out there," he said.

"I thought you wanted something from the car?"

"Do you want to go?" he asked.

"Not particularly. I want to go back to sleep. What is it?"

"There's a f***ing Dalek waiting outside the door, that's what."

Monster encounters also proved to be problematic in the hotel bar. Steve was propping up the bar waiting for me to finish my panel when he heard the manager talking to the barmaid.

"Look, it's very busy, can you work for another couple of hours?" he said in an authoritative tone.

"You what?" replied the girl.

"We're busy and you've got to cover the bar," he continued.

"Listen," she said in her barbed Scouse accent. "In the last two hours I've served three f***ing Cybermen, two Daleks and a p***ing Yeti. You can stick your job up your a***!"

And out she went! Well, Steve roared with laughter; I mean have you ever heard a more bizarre reason for walking out on your job?

There were further monster problems for another unsuspecting member of the public the following day. I had agreed to give an interview to a journalist in the foyer area, and we had not long started discussing my time on the show when a family pushed through the doors of the hotel. The father was leading, followed by the two children and a very reluctant looking mother. Her eyes darted all about her like a startled rabbit, and she began shaking in what looked like terror.

"Come on darling, they're not real," reassured the husband.

Then it dawned on me. She was scared by the costumed fans! As ever there was a Dalek patrolling the ground floor (fan Daleks still don't do stairs) and she couldn't cope with coming in close contact. Eventually she was coaxed over to reception where she checked in. My interview had gone on impromptu hold whilst I took in the scene. Looking to her right the mother spotted a pair of Cybermen walking down the stairs. That was too much for her and she took flight across the foyer and started slapping frantically on the lift button to get the heck out of there. The lift duly made a light binging noise to signal its arrival, whereupon the doors opened and out stepped a six-foot Ice Warrior. The poor lady let out a scream of abject terror, dropped her cases and hurtled out of the exit as fast as she could!

The convention circuit is, clichéd as it may sound, like one large family. Not just the *Doctor Who* part, but also the actors from the other shows you get to meet doing the big signings. Apart from the new series Doctors, I have met them all, with the exception of William Hartnell. Colin I see regularly because he's always on the circuit, Peter less so. Sylvester's lovely, and we first met at a convention where we were the only two guests. I wondered how well we'd get along, but we had an absolute ball. I know some actors don't get along with Tom, but I like him; he's just eccentric and doesn't give a damn. I knew Tom before he did *Doctor Who*, when I was living in Chelsea with Terry Longden. We frequented the same pubs, and he was quite attentive.

Someone who received a great deal of Tom's attention was Lalla Ward. She was Tom's companion in the series, and they went on to marry. I did a convention with her in the States where we shared the stage, alongside Sarah Sutton, who was Peter's assistant. Well, the three of us were chatting along quite merrily in front of the two thousand or so attendees, until the name Matthew Waterhouse was mentioned. I had never heard of him, but Lalla and Sarah had, and they slated him. I have never seen two ladies so vitriolic about one person. They went on and on. I didn't say a word, but felt my temper beginning to rise. No matter how much you dislike a fellow actor, you don't launch into a character assassination on stage before all the fans. It's just not the done thing. We finished the panel, then retired to the bar for a drink.

"How do you think that went?" asked Lalla.

"How do I think it went?" I replied, hand firmly on my drink. "I think the pair of you acted atrociously. Your behaviour was disgusting."

"What do you mean?" said Lalla, puzzled. "I don't know what you're talking about!"

"Yes you do," I continued. "When you were talking about Matthew. You should never, ever slate another actor like that; it's not professional."

Realisation dawned on the two of them.

"I'm going to walk away now," I said, "because I am so furious and need to calm down."

"I'm so, so sorry," frowned Sarah.

Sarah is a lovely girl, and I think in truth she had just been following Lalla's lead on stage. Both ladies apologised and that was the end of the matter; we were friends again. But I stand up for my principles.

Not long after, I met Matthew at a small event in Dorset. We were staying in a Travelodge, so had to use the local pub for meals. I was sitting on my own on the Saturday evening, when he came over to me.

"Hello, I'm Matthew Waterhouse," he said.

"Hello," I said, standing up to greet him.

"Can I join you, or are you like the rest of the *Who* people who don't approve of me?" he continued.

"Well I don't know you, so how could I disapprove? Sit down!"

He went on to tell me how rotten everyone had been to him on the show, and I couldn't understand why because he appeared to me a charming man.

I also got to attend a convention once in Sydney. That was a terribly long flight, with a stopover in Bangkok. I was met at the airport by Frazer and the organiser, Todd. Frazer, being Frazer, had decided to wind up Todd, and every time a little old pensioner came out pushing her cases he'd point and say: "There's Debbie!" much to Todd's horror. I had a lovely time out there, and for once got to take in all the sights, including the Opera House and Sydney Harbour Bridge. We went to Watson Bay as soon as we arrived, unpacked at the hotel, then headed out to work off the jetlag. Frazer was as always very protective towards me, making sure I was wearing sunblock and a hat, even though it wasn't really that sunny.

It's always nice to be asked to do something a little out of the ordinary at a convention, simply because it breaks the routine up a little bit. I often worry that people are tired of all the same old anecdotes, so if I can offer something a little different, I jump at it. Ian Burgess, my photographer, often puts on *Doctor Who* events, usually with a more theatrical edge. On one occasion he was organising one at the Playhouse Theatre in Weston-super-Mare. Now I'm not really a singer; I can put a song across, but I wouldn't class myself as a talented vocalist. Ian was adamant that I should sing something, and after much persuasion I agreed to perform a rendition of the great Shirley Bassey number *Big Spender*.

So I found myself rehearsing in Weston with six hunky young boys as my backing dancers. My costume left little to the imagination: leotard and tights, high heels – and lots of glittery sequins. The day of the convention arrived and I began to dread having agreed to it. I stood in the wings waiting to go on, with Sarah Sutton and Mark Strickson watching from the opposite wing, and I felt the nerves taking hold. The dry ice started, the backing track kicked in and I was on… gosh did it fly by. The final move for the climax of the number had the lads lifting me up into the air above their heads, and as they did so the place erupted in applause. I got a standing ovation; they wouldn't let me off the stage. In fact I had to do an encore! The fans were gobsmacked, and kept saying how they'd never seen me do anything like that before and how they loved the outfit. I think I proved to myself that at least I could stretch my boundaries and I'm very pleased I did it.

A year or two later I found myself back in Weston to do another show for Ian. This time in addition to *Big Spender* I performed *Cabaret*, from the musical of the same name. An added pressure was that I was being followed by a camera crew who were recording a documentary for ITV called *Landladies*, narrated by Ken Dodd, featuring different seaside towns, which would incorporate Weston and the *Doctor Who* convention. They filmed me backstage and my performance on stage, and I'm proud that there's a proper recording of it. I'm not sure I'd do it again though, but never say never…

Ian's brother Lyndsay also took a turn at running an event once, in Bristol. Lyndsay takes absolutely no prisoners, and holds no truck with the more temperamental side often shown by actors. On this occasion I was in the green room with Carole Ann Ford, as a fellow sixties girl; but she refused to move.

"I'm not going on stage until I have a pot of tea and a sandwich!" she declared.

"I'm paying you to be here," asserted Lyndsay, "so you can get on stage now, or go home without any money!"

Direct and straight to the point, but it worked. It's surprising quite how many actors will push the boundaries of what they can get out of it. If you are at an event, you are being paid and it's a professional commitment, so you do what is expected of you when you are asked.

It was around this time that I became separated from a friend of mine called Alan Langley. I'd first met Alan when he was 14 and I was appearing in a play at Poole Arts Centre. He came to the stage door with his mother to ask for my autograph. As I did more and more events so I began to see him more often, still as a fan. But as is the way with the convention family you get to know people quite well. With the number of conventions on the increase I needed help organising which ones I was doing where, and all the logistics therein, so my husband suggested Alan would be good to help. I gave him a call, we had a chat, and he agreed to manage my appearances.

Alan did a lot for me, and I'm very grateful for that. He chased royalties on *Doctor Who* pictures, suggested me as a guest to event organisers, and worked very hard in promoting me on the circuit. He would come and stop at my cottage, visit family and so on, and we had a great time together. But sadly, as time went on, the relationship began to change and I started to feel quite manipulated. He began to become very controlling over what I should wear to the appearances, how I should look, and it all became a little uncomfortable. I don't know quite what happened in the end. Alan had become very unpopular with a lot of the other *Doctor Who* actors and event organisers. Colin Baker took me aside at one in Weston-super-Mare.

"Look Debs, you're doing yourself no favours being with Alan," he said. "People dislike him and think he's overbearing. I suggest you get rid of him. And quickly."

It transpired that I had actually been losing a lot of work because he had been making demands on my behalf, demands which I simply would never have made. More money, more expenses, how long I could be interviewed for, what sort of breaks I would need… all of which painted me as some kind of diva, which wasn't remotely true.

In the end he heard from someone else that I was thinking of asking him to stop managing my appearances, and the contact was broken. No telephone call, no goodbye, it just stopped. Which was terribly sad. He did so much for me, but it had just turned sour. It didn't mean that I didn't value him as a friend any more; I'm just not the sort of person who can be controlled. Even now I cannot say that my feelings are clear over the whole incident. The last time I saw him was at a convention in Swansea where I walked out into reception and saw him talking to Steve.

"You've got longer hair," he smiled. "That's better, that suits you."

We hugged and had a drink, as if nothing had ever happened. I would like to think that we could be friends again. Maybe one day...

⁂

The convention scene nowadays is completely different to how it was when I started doing them in the eighties. Back then there was a lot of cash thrown about and huge audiences. Now they tend to be smaller in scale and fewer in number, understandably so given the harder financial times. But I prefer doing the more intimate events or the little meetings up and down the country because there's a greater opportunity to just chat to people one on one. I love asking people questions and finding out what they do. I know precisely where I get that from, because my father would always ask people "What do you do old chap?" when he met them.

I can guarantee that I will always get asked about what it was like to work with my father, or what sort of tricks Pat and Frazer played on me, and I don't mind a bit going through the stories. In fact even when I'm reluctant to do so the crowd will egg me on and get me to do it anyway. Maybe I tell the stories differently each time, or maybe people just enjoy hearing them, I don't know.

But one thing I am always reluctant to do is scream. I earned the nickname "leather lungs" on *Doctor Who* for my prodigious scream, and there was even a T-shirt made with my face and a scream written on it. The last time I did one live on stage was at a convention in America. It was a massive hall, packed full of fans, and I was doing my panel. At the end came the opportunity for the audience to ask questions.

"Miss Watling," piped up one bright spark. "Will you scream for us?"

"Pardon?" I replied.

"Well, you were renowned for your scream: will you scream for us?" he persisted.

I thought about it for a moment.

"Yes, okay I will," I smiled. "But on one condition. It's for charity. So get your money out and put it in the collection boxes!" These turned out to be a couple of buckets.

The stewards went up and down the aisles collecting money, and I began building my part up in true panto style.

"Do you really want me to scream for you?" I teased.

"Yes! Yes!" shouted the crowd.

I walked downstage to the mic, then walked back upstage, turned and teased them again:

"Are you sure?"

"Yes! Yes!" came the reply. I did this several times.

The crowd were sufficiently warmed up for the moment, so I looked up at the sound guys.

"You might want to take your earphones off," I warned.

They looked back, laughing and disbelieving.

It transpires that there was a restaurant backing onto the convention hall, and with it being Valentine's Day it was absolutely packed with loving couples having romantic meals, completely unprepared for the impending horror.

"Right, okay, on the count of three," I said, with excitement reaching fever pitch. "One, two… No, wait, let's do it the other way, three-two-one. Come on everyone."

The crowd were absolutely on the edge of their seats by now.

"Three, two, one," they chanted.

And I let out an absolute walloper of a scream.

The sound guys pulled their earphones off and cradled their ears and the crowd cheered with delight. Next door in the restaurant it was a different story. Unbeknownst to me, the scene of loving candlelit bliss had been rudely interrupted by the most violent loud scream. The diners heard this appalling noise and thought that someone was being murdered! I cleared the place entirely.

&

Not all of my convention appearances have been on dry land. I was once asked to take part in a *Doctor Who* cruise, which was organised by a man called Dan. Alan was still representing me on the circuit at the time, and he came along too, with Mary Tamm and Peter Davison. We flew out to Los Angeles where we boarded our ship, which was like a giant plastic tub – albeit one lit up like Blackpool pier.

The cabin was a tiny, claustrophobic affair. I unpacked my luggage, which was unusually plentiful. I had decided to bring along a different dress for each night, something which came as quite a surprise to Mary.

"You're going to wear something different every night?" she asked.

"Yes, I think it's nice to make an effort for the fans," I replied.

"But I don't have that many outfits with me."

"Ah," I said, "Sorry!"

I adored Peter. I had seen him at a few other events, but he'd always kept himself to himself. He wasn't shy, just a little guarded. But as we did more conventions he opened up, little by little. On the cruise the ice totally melted, and he sent me up something rotten. As is often the case!

We worked bloody hard on that cruise. There was very little downtime, and that time which we did have was still in the same areas as the fans. Which is fine, and it's what you're being paid for, but sometimes one just needs a break. The major project we undertook was to write and perform a short story. The fans were divided into three groups, one for each guest. And it worked really well. I always do my homework when reading anything. Daddy always said that the most important thing was to prepare. So I spent the next seven days looking at this story in preparation for the evening where I was going to read it out loud.

The night arrived and we all gathered together, the room full of anticipation as to how the stories would sound.

"Who wants to go first?" asked Dan.

"I will," I offered. I just wanted to get it over with, rather than sit and feel the nerves build up.

The place was so quiet during my performance. I had worked darn hard to make sure it was the best I could possibly do, and you couldn't hear a pin drop. When I finished, I left a brief pause, before looking up.

"Thank you," I said, letting out a deep breath.

The place erupted with clapping, and everyone jumped up onto their feet.

As I took my seat, Mary leaned over to me.

"I can't follow that," she whispered.

"Of course you can," I smiled.

"No I can't," she frowned. "I've only read it twice!"

I don't think Peter had even read his once. I certainly know he was a bit lax on preparation for the Big Finish audio drama we did together, *Three's a Crowd*. I was the villain, Auntie, and had some long, long paragraphs to recite. We were all in individual booths in a semicircle round the studio, like little cupboards with glass; we could all see and hear each other, but were sectioned off. Peter and I had a scene together, a pretty dark one as I recall, and at the end of it he looked over at me.

"That was pretty good, wasn't it?"

"Yes, I do hope we were pretty good together," I replied.

"No, you're pretty bloody good, aren't you?" he smiled.

The weather on the cruise was diabolical. I had packed for sunnier climes so only had two jumpers with me just in case. I practically lived in them during the day, but nothing prepared me for the rains. We had to moor up outside Catalina, and all of us (Alan, Peter, Mary and myself) agreed to meet up at the loading bay where we could get a shuttle boat to the main island. Unfortunately the bad weather really began to set in.

"I think I've left something in my room," announced Peter.

"Me too," said Mary, following after him.

"Oh, I've left something upstairs too," added Alan.

All three of them chickened out and left me. I resolved to go over to the island myself. I felt less assured when the boat hit the water and we began to rock about from side to side and up and down. It was really rough. My fellow passengers were all clinging to each other for support and at several points a number of them grabbed me to protect me. But we made it to the island eventually. As soon as we arrived, news reached us from the ship that the expedition had been abandoned because the horrendous weather was making the cruiser drag its anchor. This massive ship was being dragged inshore! They sent out tenders for those of us who'd made it over to the island, but good grief was it a rough journey back. I seriously began to question whether we'd make it or not.

Unbeknownst to me, the other three had been sitting in the bar the whole time, looking out at the weather – all concerned as to what was going to happen to me. The small boat I was on wasn't even visible through all the spray. I made it back on board, thank goodness. I was soaking wet from head to toe, and not impressed that they'd all abandoned me. I knew instinctively where they would be, and marched off to the upstairs bar. In I stormed, sodden and dishevelled.

"I've got a camcorder," smiled Peter. "Can I video you?"

"Don't start," I said, fixing him with a steely stare, and dripping copiously onto the plush carpets. "I need a drink!"

Actually I think I rather enjoyed it in retrospect. I like a good adventure!

Chapter Eleven

The first time I was asked to reprise my role as Victoria in *Doctor Who* was in 1983. The then producer John Nathan-Turner wanted to pair me off with Pat for the twentieth anniversary story, *The Five Doctors*. I would have jumped at the chance, were it not for the fact that I was already contracted to do a comedy series with Dave Allen. However, Dave had just moved from the BBC to ITV, and halfway through filming he had an argument with the producers and pulled the plug on the whole thing. I was playing all the different female characters in it, so it was going to be a great opportunity to demonstrate my acting ability, but Dave threw a wobbly and pulled the whole series. As a result I not only lost the programme, I also lost the chance to return to *Doctor Who*, and to my beloved Patrick, which was a great shame.

My other fellow actor in the Dave Allen series was Michael Sharvell-Martin, whom I went on to appear with in the West End in *Don't Dress for Dinner*. I spent three years in that at the Duchess Theatre. I used to commute there daily; up at eleven, drive to Colchester, get on the train, do the show, then do the whole thing in reverse, arriving back home at one in the morning. Sometimes I would stay in London the night before a matinee performance. For three years I repeated that pattern, until I realised I couldn't go on any longer. One morning after showering I sat on the edge of our bed, my hair up in a towel, and burst into tears.

"What's the matter?" asked Steve.

"I can't go on doing the play," I sobbed uncontrollably.

The sheer stress of the travelling and the work had taken its toll, and left me completely exhausted.

"You must get out of it now," said Steve firmly.

So the next day I handed in my notice. Unfortunately, they couldn't replace me for over a month, when a lady called Jackie Clark stepped into my role. That last month was agony to get through, so I was very relieved when it came to an end.

I had a lovely wardrobe lady called Cynthia, whom I befriended during the production. She would make sure that I had a rest before the show, and wake me up with a cup of tea. Then one afternoon she came to me with a suggestion.

"Why don't you stop over at mine?" she asked. "It will save all the commuting."

I discussed this with Steve, and he agreed it would help to cut out some of the travelling. Everything was fine for a while, but she began to get very protective of me. A little too protective in fact. She would wrap little presents for me and leave them for me to find around the flat: sometimes an item of clothing or a soft toy, or sometimes it would be a big bunch of flowers. Then she asked if she could take me to the Savoy Grill, but wanted to choose what I would wear. It was more than a little strange. She did take me out for several meals, and we got on well and laughed a lot.

When I decided to leave the show, it was in the contract that you were not allowed to tell anyone because it was against the rules of the management. On the Monday, dear Mark Furness who was the producer came into my dressing room to see me.

"So you're leaving," he said.

"Yes I am," I replied.

"Are you sure I can't persuade you to stay?"

"No, I've made up my mind, I have to go," I stated.

"Well you'll have to hold on for a while until we can replace you, will that be okay?" he asked.

Not wanting to cause them any trouble, I agreed, little knowing of the drama which was about to ensue. Cynthia found out by some means that I was leaving the cast and flew into a complete rage. She became very vitriolic and bitchy towards me.

"Why are you being like this with me?" I confronted her.

"You could have told me," she replied darkly. "Just me, nobody else. You could have told me because we're close."

Well, we weren't any more. Not after the deplorable way she'd bad-mouthed me. She spent the last month not speaking to me. It takes an awful lot to rile me, an awful lot. But Cynthia was incessant, and one day she made just one remark too many and I flew at her screaming to get out of my dressing room.

We've not spoken since.

࿇

In 1993 I was asked to attend a thirtieth anniversary *Doctor Who* convention in Hammersmith. I agreed and decided to stop for a couple of days with my sister Dilys and her son Ion, who was all of six years old, in Brixton. It so happened that it was Ion's birthday, and one of his presents was a pair of roller blades.

"I'm going to go outside and have a go on these!" he smiled, pulling the last of the wrapping off the box.

We watched him for a while, and he was very good at it. Which made me start to wonder.

"Can I have a go?" I asked, as he came to a halt in front of us.

So I put them on and started to skate along quite happily down Brixton Hill. I was doing really well until I hit a pavement slab which was slightly raised. I somersaulted forwards and landed very nastily. Auntie Debs had broken her arm, and it was now in plaster. Beyond the slight embarrassment I felt, there was the more pressing issue that in two days' time I had agreed to film a *Doctor Who* charity episode on board the Cutty Sark with Jon Pertwee.

Being the proactive type I decided to phone the costume designer.

"About my costume," I began tentatively.

"Oh don't worry, it's Victorian," he chirped happily.

"No no no, you don't understand," I stammered. "I want a cloak as well."

"A cloak?" he replied curiously.

"Yes, I need a cloak around me," I asserted.

He complied, and when the day arrived, I had a cloak on to cover up my arm. John Nathan-Turner took one look at me and said:

"What are you wearing that for?"

"Well you won't believe this, but I've broken my arm," I explained.

"What?" he exclaimed.

"It just happened…" I said, not wanting to explain the details. "So nothing too strenuous please!"

"Yes, nothing too strenuous," agreed Jon, who was playing in the scene with me.

"No, it won't be," assured JNT. "You go up the steps on the side of the ship, round the deck twice, then back down the steps and into the TARDIS."

It had began to drizzle slightly and both the wooden steps and the deck were looking dangerously slippery. The episode was being shot in 3D, so everything had to be done at a great pace with the camera swooping round in circles to get the effect.

"You can do that, can't you?" asked JNT.

"I can," I said, thinking through the moves. "But don't be surprised if I break the other arm."

It was great working with Jon, and not at all strange playing Victoria opposite a different Doctor. It felt like we'd worked together before, though we hadn't. Having done so many conventions we'd built up a friendship, which worked on screen. Jon was extraordinary at conventions because he would turn up in his full costume, with frilly shirt and velvet jacket, and a slightly regal demeanour!

I sadly didn't watch all of the Children in Need episode. From what I could tell it didn't really work, what with the addition of the *EastEnders* stuff, and the 3D element was most disconcerting. Don't get me wrong, it was lovely to be involved, and it was for charity after all; but I didn't think it was very watchable. Dear JNT tried his best and there was a heart to it, but it wasn't a classic.

A few days later I found myself at the official thirtieth anniversary event in Hammersmith. Again there were faces after faces from all eras of the show, but the one who stood out to me was Katy Manning. Now what can I say about Katy?! We never worked together on the series, but had met from time to time on the circuit, though not for a good ten years. I was sitting in the green room and she caught my eye from across the room.

"DEBBIE!" she yelled, and came hurtling towards me. "How are you?"

We exchanged pleasantries and she took my hand in hers. It seemed a bit strange, but I said nothing... but she didn't let go. She led me round the green room chatting to people, then sat next to me, and wouldn't even let go of my hand when it was time to go on. She hung on and followed me on stage! I adore her, but it did take some effort to regain my liberty.

I saw her again when I went to the convention in Australia. Katy lived over there for many years, and so she was one of the guests. I had done all of my panels during the day, and she was doing hers in the evening. I looked in on her from the back of the hall, and her head turned and she clocked me.

"DEBBIE, DEBBIE!!!" she hollered.

"Oh no, not again," I thought.

"Come on, come on stage!" she cried.

"No, no, I've done my bit," I smiled.

"Come on Debs!" she insisted.

So I went up onto the stage where she gave me a massive hug, and we continued the panel together. She's a pleasure, and totally unique. You really can't fault her for that.

⮞

My next return to the part of Victoria was to be somewhat bigger, although not necessarily more successful. Keith Barnfather called me up one day, completely out of the blue.

"Debs, I'd like you to be in a film called *Downtime*," he said, "and Victoria is the lead."

I thought it would be nice to return to the role, but then he explained that they were going to shoot it in six months' time.

"Oh no," I frowned. "I'm in *Don't Dress* for at least another year; you're going to have to count me out."

"Well, we can't do it without you because you *are* Victoria," he countered. "And we'd also like your dad back as Professor Travers."

Father had all but retired from acting by this stage, but I spoke to him and he said "Well, why not?" So I spoke to the producers at *Don't Dress* and they very kindly agreed to let me have two weeks off to film *Downtime*.

It seemed very natural to be doing it. The Yetis were there, just as they had been when I had done *Doctor Who* back in the sixties. Then there was dear Nick as the Brigadier, my dad with his white beard as Travers (no make-up required this time!), Carrie John's husband Geoffrey Beevers, and Lis Sladen back as Sarah Jane. Christopher Barry was on board as the director, having directed so many *Doctor Who*s, though not any of mine.

I read the first draft very enthusiastically, and it transpired that Victoria was now in her fifties and a power-dressing shoulder-padded university head. Great stuff. Then draft two landed on my doorstep, and it had been... altered. The production now started with Victoria, aged nineteen. NINETEEN!

I rang Keith.

"Keithy," I said. Then paused and cleared my throat. "Nineteen?"

"Yes," he replied, unfazed.

"Are you quite sure about this?" I continued. "C'mon, I'm not nineteen any more!"

"Don't worry about it, you can do it," chirped Keith.

"Well, if you say so," I said, somewhat sceptically. "Then I want the location to be somewhere very dark and very shadowy so I can get away with it."

"Seriously, don't worry!"

And so it was, a few weeks later, that I found myself lurking in the dark of the London Dungeon pretending to be a nineteen-year-old Victoria Waterfield, with James Bree as a Tibetan monk. I had a woolly hat pulled over my head and some strategically placed strands of hair, but I think I managed it.

The bulk of recording took place at Norwich University, and we were given student digs as accommodation, with little bedrooms and communal kitchens. It was basic stuff, but very jolly. Mother and Father were stopping there too, and we all used to go into the student bar at night. Daddy loved the socialising and talking to all the students.

I always had the thought in my mind that after Victoria had finished travelling with the Doctor she became a writer. She would pluck children's fantasy stories out of her mind and not quite know where they had come from, but they were all based on her time spent travelling in the TARDIS. I can picture her living alone, very quietly, in a cottage in Cornwall, having never married or had children of her own. A very insular existence. It might sound odd, but it's how I've always thought of her. That of course didn't fit in with the vision portrayed in *Downtime*, but once I started playing it, she came straight back to me. The same Victoria I had played thirty years previously was there instantly.

Whilst I don't regret making it, I don't think that it worked particularly well. It didn't make as much sense as it should have done in its own right, and perhaps tried to pack too much into seventy minutes.

The notion of Victoria having lived out her life alone was not one adopted when Big Finish came to reviving the part for one of their Companion Chronicles. The introduction makes reference to Victoria having been a grandmother, but kept the idea of her being a storyteller. The story I read was called *The Great Space Elevator*, and I thought it was a brilliant script. There's a lot of pressure on one for these audios because it's just your voice for fifty minutes, with one other actor (Helen Goldwyn in this instance) doing a few featured lines.

I live in the most inaccessible part of the country, so they very kindly put me up in a hotel the night before recording. I took a taxi to the studio in Brixton, but the driver couldn't find the studio and so he left me at the roadside. I walked up and down for a few minutes looking fruitlessly, before digging out the producer's phone number.

He didn't pick up.

"Hello, it's Watling, I'm in the street, but I don't know where you are!" I explained on his answerphone.

Undeterred, I stopped a passer-by to ask if he knew where the studio was.

"Try down there," he offered, less than helpfully.

After another half an hour or so I chanced upon the right address. It was a house with a downstairs studio. In those days I still smoked, so I had a quick cigarette to steady my nerves before going inside to meet the team, who all proved to be very friendly. Then it was into studio for soundchecks, then straight on to record. I was very worried that my voice reading alone, with no one to really bounce off, might prove boring. I think my fears were ill-founded, as the playback sounded good. The studio was booked for eight hours, but I like to remain very focused. If one takes too many breaks, it's easy to go off the boil. So we took a very quick break so the guys could have lunch (I had water because it's not very easy to do voice work on a full stomach) and then straight back onto it.

"You've got another six hours left," they said.

"I won't be here in six hours," I replied.

"You've done your homework!" they laughed.

They booked eight hours and it took me four to finish. It seems not everybody takes the time to prep and read the script thoroughly before the studio session. As an actor that is totally disastrous; preparation in advance makes your performance so much better and the production can move along so much more quickly.

"Do your homework," Father used to say. "Never ever try and bluff it."

I returned to Big Finish for a second Companion Chronicle, called *The Emperor of Eternity*. It was directed by Lisa Bowerman, who is a lovely lady and very particular about the "flow" of the storyline. After my previous troubles finding the studio, I had similar problems this time. The building was like a rabbit warren; could I find a studio? No! But eventually I made it on time. On *The Great Space Elevator* I'd had Helen, the second voice, in the studio reading with me; for this one it was Frazer, but he was recording his lines on a separate day. Lisa read in for him, although I did refuse the offer of hearing her Scottish accent! I think it worked, and I look forward to doing more in the future.

Chapter Twelve

I was rather cruelly misinformed that Balham was an up-and-coming area. Steve was still in Jersey and I had just flown back to start flat-hunting. I wanted to stay in London and saw the opportunity to make some money by investing in a property. The flat I picked out was nothing spectacular, but Steve gave it the once-over and agreed we should move in. What we didn't realise at the time was that the area was so rough, if you went out with your bag, you had to hide it under your coat. It was an evil place; and I'm hesitant to say it, but sometimes I even had to carry a knife in my back pocket for protection.

Crime was an everyday occurrence, but we'd made our bed and were forced to lie in it for the next three years. That was until one day when we pulled up outside the flat, which was on the ground floor, and realised we were being burgled. One guy was coming out of the front window and another was stuffing our VCR into a bin liner.

"They're bloody robbing us!" exclaimed Steve.

He leapt out of the car to challenge them, and one guy pulled out a large blade.

"Back off Steve, it's not worth it," I cried.

They had taken the television, the stereo... and completely trashed our home. We then had to have bars put across our windows. It was like waking up every morning in jail, and I couldn't go on living that way.

"Enough is enough, we've got to move," I declared one morning over breakfast.

I initially fancied settling in Lincolnshire, and phoned Daddy to tell him.

"We're moving," I stated on the phone.

"Where to?" asked father.

"Lincolnshire."

There was a long pause at the other end.

"Why *Lincolnshire?*" came the disdainful response.

"Because I did panto there and fell in love with the area. I've got friends there."

"No, you're not going to Lincolnshire, you're moving here to Essex," he said.

"Why?"

"Because we're here and we're your parents," he replied firmly.

I wasn't a child any more, I was a fully grown woman! Well, maybe not quite… But the more I thought about it, the more I began to think that Mother and Father were starting to get older and I would need to be nearer them.

I stayed with my parents whilst the hunt for a new home ensued, and I had three houses to view near Frinton.

"Right, we're coming with you," announced Father.

"You don't have to!" I protested.

But there was no arguing with them, and Mother and Father both duly bundled into my car to check out the said properties.

"No, no, it's not right at all," concluded Mum upon viewing the first one.

I clearly wasn't going to have much say in any of this. Off we went to the second property.

"No, you can't live here," said Father shaking his head solemnly. "It's a bit like *The Good Life* next door."

None of us liked the third option, so Mother said we should head to Thorpe-le-Soken, a small and pretty village up the road. We drove straight over and went into the tiny estate agent's on the high street.

"Do you have any cottages for sale?" asked Mother.

"It's funny you should say that," said the suited man, leafing through some papers, "but we have one just come on the market a few doors down. The owner wants a quick sale."

"How quickly?" I interjected.

"Three weeks," he smiled.

We loved the cottage on first sight. Then there was the nail-biting battle to get the mortgage sorted before the deadline; I was literally phoning the company daily, and in the end I did it with just twelve hours to spare.

Steve and I have been there for over twenty years now. It's full of happy memories; Mother and Father relaxing in the garden, barbecues in the summertime, half the village cramming into the tiny sitting room on New Year's Eve... with the fire roaring and Dad sat on the stairs asking questions for our party games. I think sometimes it might be about time to leave, but I know when I do leave the cottage it will break my heart. I romanticise about buying a flat overlooking the sea. I love the sea. I could just sit watching and listening to it for hours... with a glass of wine!

I've met so many people over the years living in Thorpe, many of whom are sadly dead and buried. When I take my dog Megs for a walk in the churchyard I find myself wandering amongst the graves, thinking about and talking to the different people I have known. It's quite extraordinary really. But there is such a great sense of community in the village. I have friends, so many friends I dare not start to list them for fear of missing someone and causing offence. They really would do anything to help each other out.

≈

I have always loved Christmas, right back from when I was a child. It was always a special time, and my parents made it that way. I hate the thought of anyone being alone over the festive period, and there were three men in the village who never had anywhere to go at Christmas: my friend Brian, who is in his seventies now and goes on a bender quite a lot, and Bernard and Roger. So I decided to have them round for Christmas dinner. I did this year in year out, but the trouble was that whilst I was cooking the turkey and trying to time all the various vegetables and puddings, they would want me to join them in the pub for a drink. I would try and squeeze in a quick one, but they would stay there for the next couple of hours. Which meant by the time dinner was ready, they were absolutely plastered. After all the effort I'd put in they might as well have been eating wood chippings! They were so inebriated that they would miss their mouths and spill food over the floor. Well, my charitable nature carried on for a few years, but eventually I had to stop. It came to a head when their table manners got so awful that Steve literally had to dash into the bathroom and throw up at the sight. From then on it was Christmas on our own!

I initially found some aspects of village life quite claustrophobic, not least the nosiness of some of the locals. Being in the acting business, I would quite often have my manager stop over, or my photographer, or whoever, just because I live so far out of London. One day a lady came up to me in the street.

"So how do you do it Debs?" she asked.

"How do I do what?"

"You've had three young men stopping here," she stated. "One on their own, then two together the other night. How do you do it? How do you pull them?"

"I don't pull them at all!" I protested.

Steve was away in Australia at the time, and she'd clearly decided I'd got a touch of the Naughty Normas.

"Come off it!" she laughed. "What's your secret?"

"It's work!" I said.

It's nice in some ways that people do take an interest, but on occasion one wonders whether the interest is a little unhealthy.

"We were very worried about you this morning," said one friend.

"Oh, why was that?"

"Well, your curtains weren't open until eleven," she continued. "Are you okay?"

"Yes I am, I just fancied a lay in!"

Quite extraordinary.

In the main, though, everybody is well intentioned. On my first day in the village I had to call upon a neighbour for help. Steve had unpacked and moved us in whilst I was away on tour, and when I arrived home on the Sunday I had no powder to wash my clothes. In the absence of a convenience store (now remedied by the dreaded Tesco Express) I went over to the pub to ask if I could borrow some. That was how I met Pete the landlord, who is a great mate to this day, and his wife Viv, who sadly passed away.

I had an unfortunate mishap with painting the exterior of my house. Being as it's a cottage I decided to have it painted Suffolk pink, and my friend Bernard agreed to do it for me. Off we went to B&Q to get it mixed and, eager to get the job finished, he started the same afternoon. I have a suspicion that the young man who mixed it for us didn't entirely know what he was doing. Suffolk pink? No. This was neon disco pink. The first coat was applied and started to get brighter and brighter and brighter... People were stopping in the street as they passed, looking at this spectacle.

"It's not my fault, honestly," I said.

Four years on, it's calmed down a little.

One very nasty experience during my time in Thorpe was my stalker. I was pottering about making the bed when I happened to glance out of the window and saw a man standing under the lamp post opposite, looking up at me. I looked away, as one does, but when I looked back he was still staring up.

Watching. I finished what I was doing, and hurried downstairs, trying to dismiss any sinister thoughts from my mind. When I got to the sitting room I looked out across the street and he was still there, staring. Eventually he disappeared, and I thought no more about it – until the next day when the same thing happened again. From then on he kept coming back. He would never come to the house, or knock at the door; he just stood watching.

I asked about him in the village. Everybody knows everybody else, so there was bound to be some clue as to who he was. It transpired he worked at the local school. We passed a couple of times in the street, and he smiled, but said nothing. Steve was away; I decided to phone him and tell him about the situation.

"You'll be all right," he laughed. "You're used to this sort of thing!"

"I'm serious, he seems a bit strange."

Steve came back shortly afterwards and we were in our local for a lunchtime drink. My stalker was sitting talking with his friend and clocked me immediately. His eyes never left me as I approached the bar.

"It's him, isn't it?" asked Steve. "The guy over there staring at you."

"Yes he is," I whispered, somewhat apprehensively.

His friend had left, so he picked up a paper and came to stand straight behind me.

"I'm going to the ladies," I said, making a rapid exit.

Unbeknownst to me, at this point Steve and his friend pulled my stalker outside and held him against the wall.

"What do you think you're playing at? Don't you ever, *ever* go near my wife again! Understand me?"

Apparently he just sort of crumpled.

I met him a couple of weeks later, while I was walking my dog.

"I'm really sorry," he pleaded. "I never meant any harm."

"You really frightened me," I said. "I had to take a carving knife to bed with me because I was scared what you might do."

"I don't know what came over me," he frowned. "I just couldn't get you out of my mind."

"Well, don't do it to anybody else," I said. "It was a horrible experience."

❧

My neighbours, H and Carol, are absolutely lovely. He's into heavy metal, but I never hear a sound. They have half a dozen chickens, so I get fresh eggs. It's country life! They start clucking at about five o'clock each morning, then the rooster kicks off to wake me up. But I love it: you really feel like you're in the heart of the country.

"Are my chickens disturbing you?" H enquired on one occasion. "Because if they are, I'll get rid of them."

"No! Don't do that, I love them," I smiled. "They're brilliant!"

The chickens aren't the only animals in my life. I have my beautiful dog Megs, who is a springer spaniel; in her senior years, but still every bit my pride and joy. I got my first dog when I was living in Balham. It was during rehearsals for *Noises Off*, performing alongside Giles, when Steve picked me up from rehearsals and told me we were going on a slight diversion.

"Diversion? What for?" I was tired and not in the mood for a diversion.

"You'll see," he grinned.

A short while later we pulled up at Battersea Dogs Home.

"I don't think he'll still be here," said Steve, getting out of the car.

"What are you talking about?"

Steve had been earlier in the day to look into buying a dog. As is sadly the way with these places, the different dogs were all jumping up and down excitedly, trying to get some attention. All bar one. A miserable looking pup who couldn't be bothered. He even had his back to the public and his head down. When we arrived at his kennel the card had been taken, so it looked as if he'd been sold. But he hadn't; so there I was on my birthday, buying myself a dog. We thought, what shall we call him? I said he looked brilliant, and Steve said he looked like a Brillopad, so we called him Brillboy!

He was such a character. He went on tour with me, and when that wasn't enough, he actually went on stage with me... and upstaged me! I remember opening in *Wife Begins at Forty* in Swansea. When the curtain went up there was dear old Jack Douglas as granddad, Brill next to him on the sofa, watching the television in the corner. I rushed in through the front door and they both turned round to look at me – much to the amazement of the audience who thought Brill was a stuffed toy! No word of a lie, Brill knew his cues. When I told him to go to the kitchen, he would bat his paws against the swing doors and exit, getting a huge round of applause every time.

One day we were doing a matinee. Now in theatre, as I have already explained, you do get the occasional nutter in the audience. It came to the part in the play where I had to go out through the doors and Brill had to follow. He took a few steps across the stage, then stopped and turned back. He was staring at someone in the front row. I followed his eyeline and clocked this extraordinary vision. She had two hats, one on top of the other, and one had a plastic fruit on it. She had a flask of tea and some sandwiches, and the most outrageous long dangly earrings, the like of which would put Pat Butcher to shame.

"Come on Brillboys, kitchen!" I commanded.

He turned back to me, took a couple of steps, then turned back again as if he couldn't believe what he was seeing. By this point we'd started to lose control on stage and began to laugh, and the audience had cottoned on and were in uproar too.

"Brillboys, *now*," I implored.

Reluctantly he came through the kitchen door and the sound of laughter was deafening.

He lived in my cottage for many happy years, and had a great life, until he became ill and had to be put down. He was twelve years old and I held him as he went to sleep. It was one of the saddest days of my life. Steve was there with me, and we just held each other and wept. People say, "Pull yourself together, he was only a dog", but he was my companion and I have great memories of him.

I thought I would never have another dog, because I couldn't bear the thought of losing it. The grief is so intense, I didn't want to put myself through the torment again. A friend of mine in the village called Peter sadly passed away after having an operation, and his son Nicko couldn't cope with looking after his dog, Megan. Nicko asked if I could possibly take her on, and I agreed.

"But I warn you," he said. "She's a man's dog, not a woman's."

A man's dog? Nonsense! She doesn't let me out of her sight and follows me everywhere in the house. She's a bit wobbly now, but I love her, and so does Steve. If we're out walking together and we have to split off, Megs will flit between the two of us, trying to herd us back together. She's very intelligent and pre-empts me sometimes. She knows when I'm about to take her for a walk and will sit waiting by the front door, and knows when I'm about to have a coffee in the garden and will sit under the table waiting. She's given me a lot of joy and pleasure, and I hope I've done the same for her.

One of the best things about my life came about by chance. Of course lots of people are aware of my theatrical background, but I had never been involved in the local amateur dramatics. Six or seven years ago Sue, the director of the local pantomime, was finding it too stressful trying to cope with the demands of running her shop and organising the show. So my doctor Alistair, who along with his wife was involved in the Thorpe Players, telephoned and asked if I could step in. I had no involvement in casting it, or even any idea which panto they had chosen, but I agreed. At least I could offer some guidance. You can't teach someone to act, but you can steer them in the right direction.

In all honesty the first panto was awful. But I've done it ever since and it has got better and better. A lot of the villagers come along to the readthrough, as we audition various people for the different parts. This year we're doing *Snow White and the Seven Dwarfs*, although Disney now have the copyright so we'll have to change the dwarf names. It's a major event locally; we get the pensioners, the kids, the parents and friends etc. Everybody comes along to watch. My stage management are brilliant and so inventive at making all the props and scenery. It's very hard work, but I look forward to it. I think if you live in a community then you have to give something back.

When the parts started to dry up, and I became disillusioned with it all and didn't want to be away from home, my husband and my family, I took to gardening. There aren't all that many parts written for older women, and whilst I'm happy to do the *Doctor Who* pieces for Big Finish, I no longer have that hunger. As an actor, if you don't have that, then it's time to stop. I was always full of confidence, but I found myself becoming less and less comfortable on stage – to the point where, midway through a performance, it just struck me that I wanted to be anywhere else rather than in front of a theatre full of people watching me. It wasn't that I had lost my nerve, just the inclination. I'd worked for over forty years as an actor, and done countless theatre productions, so it felt very strange to me to suddenly not want to do it.

My friend was setting up a gardening business, so I decided it would be fun to go in with her. We called ourselves Thyme on our Hands – quaint I know. It was successful, and then she got married and moved away, so I carried on gardening on my own. I loved it, out in the fresh air. Actually, I'm quite a fair-weather gardener. I like it when it's sunny, but if it's raining and blowing a gale, then Watling's inside.

One of the gentlemen I work for is Richard who owns Thorpe Lodge, with acres of ground around it. It's a beautiful place and he's a lovely man. Of course I work under my married name; there's no real call for a stage name in gardening, which means sometimes people don't quite make the connection as to who I am. I had worked for Richard for a few weeks when one day he came out to me.

"Debbie?" he said.

"Yes?"

"Debbie Watling?" he asked.

"How the hell did you know that?" I said, surprised.

"My wife is into theatricals," he concluded. "And she said to me, 'It's Debbie Watling doing our garden, that's Debbie Watling in our garden!'"

I laughed as he continued.

"And I used to watch you in *Doctor Who*, and hide behind the sofa."

"You're joking?" I smiled.

"You were my favourite companion in *Doctor Who* and now you're my gardener!" He was overjoyed.

So he invited me to tea so I could meet his children who also loved the show. I took along some videos for them to play and a couple of signed pictures of me as Victoria with the Daleks. *Doctor Who* gets everywhere, you can't escape it!

Chapter Thirteen

Mine, and my family's, association with Frinton Summer Theatre goes back so many years, it's very hard to do it justice. Indeed, Father took over running the theatre for many years to save it from closing, and in turn my brother-in-law Seymour took it on; all of the family have played different roles at various times over the years. Frinton Summer Theatre is a very prestigious place in the acting world; it's a weekly rep which runs annually for eight weeks, and to this day still gets thousands of applications from hopeful actors looking to launch their careers.

In a piece of dramatic irony, having made my debut on stage at Frinton, my last performance was also at the Summer Theatre. Ed, the new owner, had decided he wanted to educate the public (ha ha!) and was selecting more classically based titles to perform. One day, out of the blue, he called me up.

"I've had this wonderful idea," he enthused. "I'm doing Ibsen. Would you like to be Mrs Alving in *Ghosts*?"

"Ibsen?" I spluttered.

I didn't quite know what to say. I don't do classics; I've done thrillers and a lot of comedies, but the notion of something like Ibsen was alien to me. I've never been offered them.

"Let me think about it," I concluded.

I agreed, thinking it would be good to get back on stage, but was terrified at the prospect. I read and re-read the script; it was a huge part and I would be on stage for all but one and a half pages. Ibsen's dialogue was also quite extraordinary, with such a specific rhythm to get my head around. I learnt it all in advance of the rehearsals, because we were only going to rehearse for six days from ten in the morning 'til two in the afternoon, which didn't leave a lot of time for error. Weekly rep is terribly hard in that sense; rehearsing one play during the day, then performing another in the evening.

The day of the first performance arrived, and my mind went blank. I couldn't remember anything. I kicked myself, because I knew I had learnt it all. It came back, then it went again. The nerves were beginning to get to me; first night is always the most daunting because all of your friends come along, and the press and so forth. I made it through the dress rehearsal, then faced the prospect of what I was going to do for the three hours before the performance. I took a long walk down to the seaside to clear my head, then called back in on my mother, before returning to the theatre. One hour to go. The tension was at fever pitch. I put on my make-up and my costume, and started to get myself into character.

"Beginners please," came the call.

I stood in the wings watching. There was one short scene before I entered, and I felt my hands shaking slightly.

"Come on Watters, you've been here before, you can do it," I told myself.

On I went... and I made it through. The first night was a bit of a blur. But Mother and Steve were both there to support me, and I think my performance got better as the week went on and I became more comfortable doing it. There was one minor blip where I completely forgot what I was saying and began to ad-lib. Well, you try ad-libbing Ibsen: it's not easy, I can tell you. I went downstage and started to thump my hand against the wall, which (being a Frinton set) wasn't the wisest of moves. However, the line shot back into my head, and I managed to carry on as if nothing had ever happened. The relief on my leading man's face was quite something. By the time we reached the last performance, I thoroughly enjoyed it... maybe because it was the last one!

I also directed a few productions at Frinton. I don't know quite how that came about, but I think it was suggested by someone whilst Father was running it with Giles. I had worked with enough directors over the years, I had a fair idea of what to do, so thought there would be no harm in giving it a go. The biggest problem was blocking characters on paper so that their movements didn't cross, something further compounded by the minimal size of the stage at Frinton. The first production I directed was Alan Ayckbourn's *Absent Friends*. There's something very rewarding about watching the play come together and start to click. I have always been more of a guider than a director.

"Have you thought about doing it like this?" I would offer. Or "Have you tried doing it this way?"

This is more likely to get a better result out of an actor than telling them exactly what you want them to say and how you want them to say it. Let them pick it up from your suggestions, and run with it. It also helps if your director is an actor too as they will understand your problems much earlier on.

One time I was assigned to direct *Don't Dress for Dinner*, and the leading girl in it had done five plays in a row. That's five different plays with completely different styles over five weeks, which is tough. She walked into the rehearsal room on the Monday morning and burst into tears; she'd hit the mental barrier.

"Ten minute break," I called, and took her outside.

"I can't do it," she wept. "But I can't let everyone down."

"Look, you're not letting anyone down," I comforted. "This is how it gets in weekly rep; it's hard."

I had played the same part in the West End version, and agreed to relearn the script. If she still didn't feel up to it by Saturday, then I said I would go on in her place. I knew that would work. As an actress you never want someone else taking over your part. When we came to the dress rehearsal she was word perfect.

ॐ

Having made my last stage appearance in Ibsen, my last television appearance was at the opposite end of the scale.

"They want you to do this thing called *Identity*," said my agent. "It's hosted by Donny Osmond."

"What is it?" I asked.

"It's filmed in Manchester and it's a quiz show," he explained.

I wasn't convinced it was going to be any good. The premise was that there are a number of people lined up stood on pedestals and then there are a selection of professions; Donny gives the contestants clues and they have to match the profession on the board to the person on the pedestal. Very strange.

"Well, she's got boots on," reasoned Elaine, the contestant. "But she looks too frail to be a jockey."

It's an odd sensation being stood on a pedestal for a long period of time; you begin to lose balance, and a few of the people did. Given the varied heights at which we were stood, I can only imagine the injuries which might have befallen some of the victims.

Every few clues the contestant would have to guess who we were.

"I think number three is the baker."

"Are you sure?" Donny would ask in the most unsettling of tones.

"Yes, definitely, he's the baker," they would resolve.

The music would begin slowly, then crescendo to a climax, whereupon number three would reveal whether they were a baker from Romford or a nuclear physicist from Droitwich. Mercifully I was picked out halfway through the show, and escaped both my pedestal and the inane questioning.

"Dear Elaine, I won't exterminate you… yes, I am Doctor Who's assistant."

And with that I was off.

I watched the show back, and it was so frighteningly mundane. I was in the kitchen, and Steve was watching it.

"Come on Debs," he called.

"No, I don't want to see it," I said, peeling the carrots.

"Don't be daft!"

I poked my head round the door, and eventually sat down to watch. What I hadn't banked on was quite how many people in the village would see it. Who knew how many of them were sat at home in the afternoon watching television?

"You didn't tell us you were on *Identity* with Donny Osmond!" they chided.

"I didn't think anyone would be very bothered," came my retort.

All that fuss over an afternoon quiz!

I have been asked to do a few DVD commentaries for different productions. I've done some for *The Invisible Man*, and a couple for *Doctor Who*, though sadly not as many as I would have liked because the BBC wiped so many! It's very different watching a programme and having to talk over it. The first one I was called upon to do was *The Tomb of the Cybermen*, with Frazer.

"How can you remember so much of this, it was years ago?" puzzled Frazer during a coffee break.

"Because I watched it last night you fool, to jog my memory!"

"I should have done the same thing," he muttered.

Even though it's not acting, you still have to prepare! But we were very good together; we still have the chemistry and can bounce off each other with different memories and stories. I remember we were both interviewed for a documentary in 1993 to celebrate the show's thirtieth anniversary, and they used an elaborate reconstruction of the Emperor Dalek set as the backdrop. When it went out they'd cut all of Frazer's responses, but mine were intact! Frazer phoned me up saying how stupid he thought he'd looked, just sat there watching me speak. It was a shame all the footage had gone to waste.

Right towards the end of the commentary, because he has a reputation for being slightly tight-fisted, I decided it was time to set Frazer up. The end credits were drawing near and we were beginning to wind the whole thing up.

"I think that went well," I started.

"Yes, me too," agreed Frazer.

"Then I think we need a drink in the bar," I said. "And you're paying!"

Frazer's jaw dropped, and the recording stopped.

"You little sod," he protested.

"I know," I laughed. "I've been waiting years to do that."

Daddy hadn't been very well for a long time by this point. When I agreed to do the commentary, they offered to send a car to get me there and back. I was on the way home when my mobile went off. It was Vanda, Giles's wife.

"I think you'd better get to the hospital straight away," she said. "Your father is fading."

I knew that once the car dropped me off at home, it would still be another hour to drive to Daddy, and I was in a terrible state. The mobile went again.

"He's improving now, Debs," said Vanda. "Don't worry about it."

"Are you quite sure?" I didn't want to take any chances.

"Yes, yes, don't worry, honestly," she reassured.

I got home, went into my cottage and the phone went once more.

"Sorry," said Vanda. "You'd better get here now."

I threw myself into the car and raced to the hospital. Mummy was in the waiting room with Nicky and Giles. Father had had a bad turn, but then he recovered from it, and they moved him to a side ward. It began to look like he was going to start getting better. But then he had another turn, and we began to realise that we were going to have say goodbye to Daddy.

We stopped the whole night with him, and he made it through. After a week or so they moved him to a care home in Frinton to monitor his progress and let him recuperate, and we would all visit daily. He was the most extraordinary character; he had a lot wrong with him, but he would still want to be out and about, and Mother would push him up and down in his chair. One day I turned up to visit and he was sitting by his bed playing chess with Giles. They had a very close relationship and would often play chess. The pair of them each had a Scotch in hand, and I sat on the bed. It looked so normal.

Then I got the call that he was going to have to be moved back to hospital, because his condition had deteriorated. When I arrived at the hospital he was unconscious. The doctor explained that they had put him on morphine and that, if he did recover, he would be a vegetable.

"No, we can't have him like that," said Giles.

Father was such a strong, proud man; there was no way we could let him lose his dignity.

Giles was due to start rehearsals in a play with Kate O'Mara the next day, so he went home to pack. Nicky needed a break, so she too went home. This left Mother and myself at Daddy's bedside. And we sat there for another couple of hours, and just watched him go. It was very quiet, and very peaceful. Just a light sigh, then he was gone.

The doctor came in and said what a wonderful man he thought Father had been, quite the gentleman and how courteous he was to all the staff. We listened to him, still numb, then turned to Daddy to kiss him goodbye. It had only been a matter of minutes, but he was already stone cold.

Out in the corridor I phoned Nicky to tell her. She dashed straight back, and I couldn't believe what she did. She's very heavily into her religion, but I wasn't quite prepared for her reaction.

"Hallelujah!" she cried as she burst into the room, raising her arms. "He is free!"

I rang Giles, and he said he wasn't going to come to the hospital. He wanted to carry on and just remember Father as he was, which I understood completely. I think it was quite a relief when he did pass away; we were all expecting it, but not knowing when it was going to come. It sounds an awful thing to say, but when someone you love so much is suffering, you just want them to be free of it. Mercifully, now he was.

Chapter Fourteen

Dilys flew the nest when she was about seventeen; she left home and moved into a flat with another girl in London. Her first job was at Raymond's Revue Bar, the notorious venue for strip tease. It was tradition in our family that we would go along and offer support on first nights, no matter how bad the production, or in this case, regardless of the venue. Daddy was taken aback when she told him about her new job, but we all came along to see her and offer some support, including Nan. We saw many sights and wonders that night, not least a young lady with a most unusual trick involving a very large snake. We were all a little apprehensive as to what Nan's response would be. Would she be shocked or outraged by the spectacle before her? All eyes turned to her for her reaction at the end of the night.

"Well", she said, "it's all very well these ladies stripping off, but why were there no naked men?"

Dilys was always very successful in musicals and comedies, although she did do a short stint as a regular in *Coronation Street*. When she played Broadway in *Promises Promises* she was even nominated for a Tony Award. Whilst she was always very successful on stage, she did have her fair share of unfortunate relationships off. Her first husband, an Australian called Bruce, was an utter bastard to her. However, she met a lovely guy called Chris Matthews on tour, and they married. It was Chris who created my family nickname, which for the record is "Donks". I came home from tour one day and quite out of the blue he said:

"Oh Debbie Donks, welcome back, how are you?"

"What's the Donks about?" I said, eyeing him curiously. "It sounds like a donkey!"

But it's stuck ever since.

Dilys and Chris were together for about eleven years, and had a son called Sam, who was born with water on the brain. Sadly he passed away when he was four months old; he was in Great Ormond Street Hospital, but there was nothing they could do. It broke Dil's heart; in fact it broke all our hearts.

Chris had a son and a daughter from a previous marriage, and the daughter Susie used to come to Frinton and visit us. One day we were playing down on the beach and I marked out a hopscotch in the sand.

"I can't do it," she said with a concerned look on her face. "I can't jump."

I knew something was wrong. Sadly she ended up in a wheelchair, unable to speak and fed through a tube. She lived on for a few more years, but passed away shortly after her twenty-first birthday. Chris's son Luke got leukaemia when he was sixteen, but thankfully recovered from it. In fact he was a pageboy at my first wedding.

Dilys was on tour in *Rattle of a Simple Man* when she met a young Welsh lad by the name of Owen Teale. He was years younger than Dil, but they fell madly in love, married, and had a son together called Ion, who has grown up into a fine young man. Owen used to come down to Frinton a lot and became an important part of the family, which makes it such a pity that I don't see him any more. He remarried after he and Dil got divorced, and is now with another actress, Sylvestra Le Touzel. Ion went to live with them and their two daughters, because sadly Dilys became an alcoholic. I would stop with her sometimes when I was in the West End, and come back at night to see her passed out on the sofa, with Ion, who was all of four, crying and trying to drag her to bed. It hasn't damaged him, and he's grown up into a very sound, sensible, fun-loving man. But Dilys was always quite a heavy drinker, and one day something just tilted.

"It's either your son, or the bottle," I told her.

She sadly chose the bottle. Ion wouldn't have dealings with her for many years, but now he's in his twenties he sees her regularly. He takes his girlfriend along, and I think some inroads have been made into repairing the damage that was done.

There was never any real rivalry between myself and Dilys. People would often ask about it, but as a family we were always off doing different things; it was never really something we thought about. The only time I can recall seeing Dilys look a little affronted was when I went back to the Hall to tell them that I had got the lead in *The Wednesday Play*. There was just a little pause, and a look that crossed her face. She was doing very well in the West End, but there was just a slight feeling that little seventeen-year-old me shouldn't be getting the big roles just yet. But she was always terribly fond of her little sister, as I was of her. I would go and stop at her flat in London, and we'd put on make-up and do all the girly things together.

There was one occasion when this backfired, however. Dil decided it would be a good idea to use one of those home dyeing kits to make me blonde; sadly she didn't do it properly and my hair turned a very bright shade of ginger. Actually, not so much ginger, more carrot. I had to travel back home, and then explain to Mummy and Daddy what had happened. They were not best pleased!

❧

One day when I was working at The Pink Clock, the phone rang.

"Is that Deborah Watling?" asked the voice on the other end.

"Yes, who wants to know?"

"You need to get over to Whitcross Hospital as soon as possible."

"Why?" I asked.

"Your Mother has been involved in a car accident."

I knew she'd set out that morning in her green Mini to visit Dilys in St John's Wood in London for lunch, but I didn't have any idea as to what could have happened. I was the first person they could reach and I tried not to panic, heading straight over to the hospital. When I got there the curtains were drawn round Mother's bed. I dew them back and the sight which met my eyes was terrible. Her face was slashed down one side, covered in blood and bruises. I hardly recognised her. It transpired that she'd been at the traffic lights, they turned to green and she continued her journey and was hit by a truck which had overshot the lights.

"How old are you?" asked the matron.

"What's that got to do with anything?" I said in shock. "Twenty-two."

"That's all right then," she said looking down at her clipboard.

"What's all right then?" I demanded.

"We need your permission," she said.

"Permission for what?"

"Either we leave your mother here, and she will certainly die, or…" She paused. "Or we take her down to the operating theatre and she will probably die on the way. What do you want us to do?"

"There's no option," I stressed. "You take her down for the operation and I shall hold her hand all of the way."

I was in the side room for hours, just waiting. It seemed like an eternity. Daddy was filming *The Power Game*, and he got a telephone call at the studio to give him the news. He came straight over, and I told him exactly what had happened; then it was just a question of counting the minutes.

"Right then, where's the nearest pub," said Dad. "We need a drink."

He wasn't being callous. We were badly shaken and there was nothing we could do waiting in that gloomy side room. Father wasn't a great one for expressing his emotions: he'd tended to keep his feelings to himself. But I could tell he was affected deeply.

She didn't die, but it took four months for her to recover. She even had a relapse, which was terrifying. It was a terribly stressful time. Mummy had always been there for us, so the prospect of losing her was one I couldn't even contemplate.

Father's death had a terrible impact on all of us, but Mother especially. She went to pieces, and came to live with me for a few weeks. We took a short holiday abroad to get away from it all. What I didn't realise was that she'd started drinking heavily to overcome the grief. I can understand why: she'd been married for fifty-four years, and had just lost her soulmate. She would literally start drinking at ten in the morning. She had a breakdown, and was hospitalised for a while. The family rallied round, and we brought in a carer, Sandra, who has been with Mother ever since.

It turned out that Mother had been taking complete strangers into her home, just to talk to them because she was so lonely. And to show how deeply despicable the human spirit can be, some had taken advantage of her and her money. She really was a lost soul for a very long time. But we all persevered, and she pulled through.

She's now a contented lady of ninety years of age, as she will tell anyone with absolute glee. It's funny that for so many years she was very sensitive about her age and birthdays, and is now delighted to be so much older than anyone else she meets. She has her little dog, a white fluffball by the name of Millie, and spends her days relaxing at home or walking out in the fresh sea air.

৵

Giles was always something of a tearaway in his youth. He used to run away from school so often that it seemed we spent more time taking him back there then he did actually taking any lessons. When he left school he didn't go to drama school; instead, he went straight into the business, helping Father with Waltham Forest Theatre, appearing in a few productions and doing some stage management.

I recall one of his earliest roles was in *Upstairs Downstairs*, looking terribly young in a kilt, as a friend of Simon Williams. He went on to help Daddy run Frinton Theatre. Father didn't want to deal with the paperwork side, so Gizzy handled it for him. Eventually he took over, and then his career took off. He did a few parts in the West End, and then found wider fame playing the vicar in the BBC sitcom *Bread* by Carla Lane. Nowadays he lives in Frinton, with his wife and two beautiful girls: twins, who are now in their teens. Both of them want to go into the business, one as an actress, and one on the stage management side. And so the Watling tradition goes on!

Of course, since Father's death, Giles is now head of the family. He's done repairs on Mother's house, and handles all her affairs, as well as trying to organise everyone else's!

"Everything all right Debbie Donks?" he'll ask. "Anything I can help you with?"

"No no, I'm quite all right," I reply.

"Well, if there's anything you need to know don't hesitate."

It's very strange; he was the little boy I used to drag up Alderton Hill by his satchel, berating him and calling him a lazy little sod! Now both he and his wife are very respectable councillors. He still writes plays, as well as directing, and acts from time to time when he can fit it in. Giles looks so much like Father when he walks into the room; his hands are exactly the same, it's like looking at Daddy's hands. He's very contented with his life, and his two girls, who are straight-A students. They were always inquisitive and hungry to learn more, and he was a great father and encouraged them wherever possible.

I feel in many ways that I sort of brought up my younger sister, Nicky, who is ten years my junior. She's now happily married to Seymour, and they have three kids. She tried entering the business, but didn't really get on with it.

I remember one funny instance where we both auditioned for a television series down in London. I must have been twenty-five, but I was up for the part of a fifteen-year-old girl. I walked in and they asked me to take my make-up off. They looked me over and decided I was right, and I got the role. Two days later Nicky auditioned for the other sister, who was eighteen, and she got that part. So we were playing sisters, but the wrong way round! Unfortunately the series was cancelled, which was a shame as it would have been great to work alongside Nick-Nack. She's very artistic and makes lots of wonderful pictures and sculptures. She is also very strongly into her religion, and has a great faith which she has brought her two daughters up to follow.

I am living very contentedly in my cottage now, with my husband Steve, and my dog Megs. Steve and I lived together for many years before marrying, and he actually went down on one knee eight times before I caved in. We decided on a very quiet, small ceremony in a registry office in Colchester, with just immediate family; his parents and mine, and so forth. I stopped with Mother and Father the night before, sticking to the traditional belief that you shouldn't see the groom before the day of the wedding. I thought this was ridiculous as we'd been co-habiting for eight years, but went along with it all the same. The next morning I made my final preparations in the mirror; hair up and in place, make-up ready. Then I went out to the car, and we set off; Mummy and Daddy in the front, me in the back.

We hadn't driven far when Mother suddenly let out a gasp of horror.

"Oh no! My earrings!" she cried. "I've forgotten to put them on, we must go back!"

"It's my wedding day, we're going to be late!" I protested.

"No, Jack, turn back," she was adamant. "I can't go to the wedding without my earrings."

So we had to go back to find her earrings, then set out again. Eventually we arrived at the registry office and pulled into the car park. I looked out of the window, and there were loads of people stood around. Stranger than that, I recognised most of them. Half the village had turned out for the wedding! Dad got out of the car with Mummy, and everybody went into the registry office. Except, of course, for me. I was still sitting in the back of the car! I twiddled my thumbs for fifteen minutes, expecting someone to collect me at any moment.

Inside the registry office, one individual had noticed my absence, and approached Father.

"Haven't you forgotten something?"

"No," said Father, somewhat bemused. "What have I forgotten?"

"Are you sure you've not forgotten anything?" they enquired.

"What on earth do you think I've forgotten?" retorted Father.

"The bride?"

Having finally been collected, I walked in for the ceremony, and the hall was packed. At the end everybody cheered, and we received a huge round of applause.

A fantastic surprise awaited my return home: the cottage was bedecked in bunting and balloons, with massive congratulations banners hoisted up in the air. The whole village had clubbed together to make a beautiful spread, and there was champagne galore for everyone from the pub's cellar. Everything was going fine, in fact, until I lost Steven. I asked around as to where he had gone.

"He's gone to the pub to fetch some more champagne," said Dilys.

"The pub? Has he now?"

I marched across the road in full wedding gear and into the pub, where Steven was seated at the bar, drinking a pint of Guinness and chatting to one of the locals.

"Steven!" I barked.

He dropped his pint down onto the counter.

"Our guests are all parched, waiting for you to come back with the champers," I ranted. "So I suggest you get your butt over the road with some more bottles!"

We'd only been married an hour, and there I was already tugging the ball and chain!

That was seventeen years ago, and we have a friend called Roger who every year used to send us an anniversary card. A couple of days before he'd ring up and say:

"Debs, you know it's your anniversary in two days' time, don't forget."

I'd thank him, then rush out to buy a card. It turns out he would do the exact same thing for Steve. He's a bit old now and no longer sends us a card, so we never remember our anniversary. The only date we do with any certainty is Christmas. We don't even do birthdays any more, as neither of us can stand them at our time of life.

Steve actually had his mid-life crisis when he hit thirty-nine. I took him breakfast in bed and he was in a terrible mood. He didn't want to get up, and when we went out for dinner that evening he didn't want to talk. When a guy looked at me in the bar he flew into a rage and threatened to punch his lights out. This just wasn't in keeping with his character! So I took him home and gave him a severe talking-to, before banishing him to the spare room. The next morning he was a reformed character, full of the delights of spring. Anyway I won't throw too many stones, in case he decides to reveal what I was like on my sixtieth birthday…

We've had more than our fair share of obstacles and trials, Steve and I; but we have stuck together throughout them, we're still together, and still very happy to this day.

Epilogue

What do you say about a man you've known all your life? Someone you've adored? I mean my father, Jack. We had a rather special relationship from when I was born, because I was his first-born. He always encouraged me to do things, to push myself further.

He helped me through my dyslexia; when he was doing *The Power Game* I would come home from school and he'd say to me:

"Come on Debbie, let's go through my lines."

And I would go white. I knew something was wrong with me; I couldn't read properly. I used to sit down and he would make me read. That helped me a lot.

He was a very kind man, a very gentle man, of the old school. One of his traits, which was absolutely wonderful, was that he was always very interested in other people, and would always ask what they did. If ever anyone came up to him in the street and said:

"Hello Mr Watling, we saw you on the telly last night and thought you were very good."

He would say:

"Thank you very much. Now what about you? What do you do?"

I think that I've inherited that trait.

I was there, with Mother, on the day he passed away. Just the two of us together in that room, sitting with him.

That was nine years ago.

As I write this, I am sitting in the dining room of our family home in Frinton-on-Sea. In Father's chair. I shall always remember him with great affection, as will all of the family. He was a huge part of my life. Daddy is buried in a small church on the seafront, a very old church, and I sometimes visit him there. Not very much, because I do tend to break down. But I suppose he still lives on in his children. And I think of him every day. You have to come to terms with the death of a loved one, but I shall never forget him.

He's with me every day, my father.

JACK STANLEY WATLING
13th January 1923 – 22nd May 2001

Also available from

MARY TAMM

First Generation

THE AUTOBIOGRAPHY

In the 1970s, she travelled the universe aboard the TARDIS… 30 years on, actress Mary Tamm now recounts the story of her own, earthbound, adventures.

Born to Estonian parents in 1950s Bradford, her rise to fame took her from a Northern childhood to life in the fast lane: via TV appearances in *Coronation Street* and *The Girls of Slender Means* to leading roles in feature films – including the cult *Tales that Witness Madness*, and *The Odessa File* which pitched her career into the international arena.

In 1978, Mary became part of essential Saturday night television as she joined the cast of *Doctor Who* alongside Tom Baker, as the superlative Time Lady, Romana!

Packed with recollections and exclusive photographs, this autobiography follows Mary on a journey of self-discovery to her parents' homeland of Estonia, where she finally comes to terms with her true identity…

ISBN 978-1-906263-39-3

Available in paperback and audio from
www.fantomfilms.co.uk